A CELEBRATION OF
COOKING
IN AMERICA

Timeless Recipes from the Kitchens of Pet

PET
An **IC Industries** Company

B
BENJAMIN

Produced and Published by: The Benjamin Company, Inc.
                          One Westchester Plaza
                          Elmsford, New York 10523

The following trademarks appearing in this centennial cookbook are owned by
and identified products of PET INCORPORATED, ST. LOUIS, MO 63102 (An IC
Industries Company): **PET, OLD EL PASO, NACHIPS, COMPLIMENT,
HEARTLAND, SEGO LITE, AUNT FANNY'S, UNDERWOOD, B&M, AC'CENT,
ORLEANS, WHITMAN'S, PET-RITZ, PET WHIP, DOWNYFLAKE.**

Cover printed by McGrew Color Graphics — An IC Industries Company
ISBN: 0-87502-133-6
Library of Congress Catalog Card Number: 84-072096

Printed in the United States of America
First printing: December 1984

CONTENTS

INTRODUCTION

Americans always seem to be celebrating. Holidays, birthdays, anniversaries, weddings, housewarmings, football games, baseball games — almost every special event turns into a good reason to get together and have a celebration.

Celebrations and good food just naturally go together. And for nearly all of our history, whenever and wherever families and friends have come together for special occasions, Pet has been there. This year, we at Pet are having an important celebration of our own — our 100th anniversary. And we would like you to join in our celebration through this collection of timeless recipes from our own Pet Kitchens.

Since 1885 Pet has been providing wholesome, high-quality food and recipes for the American consumer — for you, your parents, your grandparents, maybe even your great-grandparents. So this book also will take a step back in time to celebrate 100 years of cooking in America. We'll be exploring our roots and taking a look at the changes time has wrought in all our lives. And we'll see how Pet has grown and changed along with our great country.

The Great "Cooking Pot"

One of the wonderful things about American food is its almost infinite variety. People from many lands settled in the U.S., bringing different tastes and unique cooking styles and adapting both to native American food. So many cooking styles evolved that even today, when many of the same fresh and frozen foods are marketed from coast to coast, distinctive regional tastes and customs prevail.

The New England Yankees cherish their creamy fish chowders, their baked beans and brown bread, their seafood fresh from the tidal flats. When they throw a party, it's often a clambake, with clams and other shellfish steaming in seaweed packed on heated rocks.

The barbecue was popularized in the Old South, but its roots trace back to the American Indian, who roasted whole pigs over hickory coals as the central offering of a huge "picnic." Today, under the Texas sun, the favorite meat is a whole steer on a spit, and spicy barbecue sauces run extra hot.

What we call Southern cooking hasn't any one character, but is instead an enchanting potpourri of Anglo-Saxon, Latin American, and African traditions. In Virginia and the Carolinas, that might mean country hams, fried chicken, hot biscuits, and pecan pie. The cooking styles of Creoles and Cajuns are influenced, on the one hand, by the cuisines of French and Spanish ancestors, and on the other, by French peasant cookery filtered through a stay in Nova Scotia — all enhanced by the spices and traditions of Africa.

From the thrifty Pennsylvania Dutch (mostly *Deutsch*, or German), come such dishes as scrapple, Philadelphia pepper-pot soup, and shoofly pie. While those specialties have tended to remain regional delights, their apple butter has won favor far and wide.

The festive smörgåsbord was the gift of Scandinavians who settled in Minnesota and the Dakotas. Their "bread and butter table" might offer lutefisk, lefse, meatballs, and Krumkaker, but the term has expanded to include any lavishly spread buffet table.

A few food-centered celebrations are so distinctly American that they flourish from coast to coast. The tailgate party could exist only in a society that lives on wheels. The cocktail party has been around, in one form or another, for centuries. With the creation of tempting appetizers and hors d'oeuvres, Americans have raised this special branch of cooking to an art form.

6

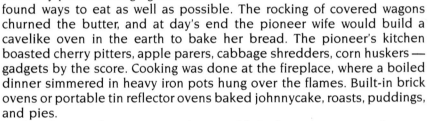

Louis Latzer

A Century of Change

American ingenuity has always come up with ways and tools to do the job faster, better, and more easily. Even the early pioneers forging westward found ways to eat as well as possible. The rocking of covered wagons churned the butter, and at day's end the pioneer wife would build a cavelike oven in the earth to bake her bread. The pioneer's kitchen boasted cherry pitters, apple parers, cabbage shredders, corn huskers — gadgets by the score. Cooking was done at the fireplace, where a boiled dinner simmered in heavy iron pots hung over the flames. Built-in brick ovens or portable tin reflector ovens baked johnnycake, roasts, puddings, and pies.

The nineteenth century woodstove with its hot-water reservoir was a marvelous innovation. While the housewife banked her cookfire with a poker and hoped the heat would hold long enough to bake a cake made with "a handful" of this, "the size of a walnut" of that, and "a heaping spoonful" of something else, she stood on the threshold of a century of phenomenal change.

The gas range was just around the corner, and after that the electric range. Then would come electric fry pans, toasters, broilers — all sorts of specialized appliances. Mixers, blenders, and food processors would speed food preparation, and microwave ovens would turn the work of hours into minutes. Refrigerators and home freezers would preserve fresh food for days and months.

In the midst of this great century of evolution in cooking came Pet. We started as a small company in the midwestern town of Highland, Illinois, across the Mississippi from St. Louis, Missouri. In those pre-refrigeration days, milk was transported by horse-drawn wagons over bumpy dirt roads, and it might not be in top condition when it reached the city. The only sure supply of pure milk was a cow close at hand. Our dream was to put cans of clean, fresh milk — milk that would keep indefinitely — on the pantry shelf of every American home.

Dedication, and a Dream

The name Pet came years later. At first, we called ourselves Helvetia Milk Condensing Company after the Swiss farming community (Helvetia is Latin for Switzerland). John E. Meyenberg, a young Swiss, brought from his homeland the idea behind condensing and preserving milk without the use of sugar. The original process had its flaws, and when Meyenberg left the company, the remaining investors, led by Louis Latzer, were determined to perfect Meyenberg's evaporation and canning processes. At last, after many years of experimentation, they succeeded. Pure milk could now be stored indefinitely without fear of spoilage.

With Latzer as president, our little company prospered. The growing success of "Evap" led to the introduction of many brand names. But our most popular brand was "Our PET," introduced around the turn of the twentieth century as a baby-sized can that sold for five cents. In time it became so popular that we took the name of our brand and became the *Pet Milk Company.*

Our evaporated milk had become a major food product, and American consumers were finding more and more uses for PET Milk. Babies thrived on it, and mothers found its consistent, rich texture perfect for cooking. From our earliest days we created recipes for Pet customers, sometimes printing them on can labels, later offering recipe brochures and cookbooks. Our libraries at Pet headquarters overflow with early recipe collections offering advice and information that, while vital to the early 1900s homemaker, seem quaint today. One early cookbook gave these instructions for preparing PET Milk for whipping: *Strip label from the can and place it on a block of ice ... let it stand overnight.* In the days before electric refrigeration became common, that was the best way to chill food.

Food preparation techniques have changed, but many of the recipes found in those early cookbooks, like the famous 75-year-old Pet recipe for Pumpkin Pie, have probably remained a part of your own family's traditions.

Spreading the Word

Today every company advertises, but back in our early years a product relied heavily on word-of-mouth to tell the world of its quality and convenience. After the Spanish-American War, for example, soldiers and sailors, impressed with the handy canned milk that stayed fresh even in the field, took the news of the "tin cow" home, and Pet's sales soared.

"We look upon advertising much as we do upon marriage, a thing not to be entered into hastily nor cast aside easily," Pet told retailers in the early twentieth century. Our early ads were called "grandmotherly," but a dynamic advertising executive, Erma Proetz, took charge in the 1920s, advancing the art of advertising and putting PET Evaporated Milk on the national scene. Her full-color, full-page magazine ads pictured warm, happy family groups and young, stylish women. "Take Baby and Go" proposed one of her award-winning ad campaigns, and the idea was a revelation. Portable, fresh, reliable, PET Evaporated Milk was helping lend a little extra mobility to the American family as the country entered the automobile age.

Even our earliest ads included simple recipes — how to mix PET Milk with orange juice for the "perfect drink"; how to cook meat in milk for a "cream and butter flavor." Mrs. Proetz also established our first test kitchens and created a spokesperson for the powerful new medium of radio. For twenty years, our Mary Lee Taylor talked over the airwaves every Saturday afternoon, bringing recipes and nutrition information to thousands of listeners across the nation. Her program was one small part of something that's been central to our philosophy from the earliest days: an unwavering commitment to providing education and assistance to the people who buy our products.

Branching Out

A healthy, mature company, Pet was expanding. Our headquarters moved to St. Louis, and we built dozens of milk condensaries throughout the East, the Midwest, and the South. Where we found no ready sources of milk, we helped local farmers develop dairy stock and pastures. When the new dairy farmers produced an overabundance of fresh milk, we found other uses for it. Starting with ice cream, we built a fresh dairy business that today thrives in America's southeastern states.

Expansion into western markets received a boost in 1925 when Sego Milk Products Company of Utah joined the Pet family. And we developed our first powdered milk for the bakery trade.

But it wasn't until after World War II that we took the big step of broadening our horizons into nondairy fields. In the postwar years, evaporated milk sales began to decline. Prosperity had put a refrigerator in every kitchen, fresh milk was widely available, infant feeding formulas were becoming more prevalent, and canned milk was heading for the back shelf. Our management knew that it was time to diversify, to search for new ideas and new products to serve changing consumer needs.

Milk . . . and More

In 1955 we welcomed an important newcomer to the Pet family — a small frozen pie business with the curiously similar name of Pet-Ritz. Our adoption of that promising little company was our first venture into nondairy foods, signaling a whole new direction for Pet's future.

We admired the Pet-Ritz products and recognized two important needs of the busy American homemaker. She wanted to serve her family the best-tasting pies . . . and she was always looking for ways to save time and effort in the kitchen. With our PET-RITZ frozen pies and pie shells, we've been able to help her meet both those needs.

In 1963, we added another emerging frozen food business — Downyflake Foods, Inc., makers of frozen donuts and waffles. Today, both PET-RITZ and DOWNYFLAKE are nationally known brands, and are two of the most popular product lines in the rapidly growing frozen foods market.

Another fine food company came under our wing in the 1960s — the prestigious Whitman's candy company, maker of America's favorite boxed candy, the WHITMAN'S SAMPLER. Whitman's has been a part of the American scene even longer than Pet, and the happy marriage of all those years of experience in bringing people the products they love has let us create together a constantly expanding line of popular confections.

Old El Paso was canning Mexican foods long before the trend swept the country. In 1968 the respected southwestern firm became another promising addition to the Pet shelf of fine food products. By introducing our customers to many zesty new flavors — all in convenient, easy-to-prepare form — we've helped whet the growing national appetite for good Mexican food.

By the time Old El Paso came to Pet, we had dropped the "Milk" from our name to become Pet Incorporated. That move reflected our new commitment to providing a whole family of quality food products ... SEGO diet foods, HEARTLAND cereals, DOWNYFLAKE frozen waffles, COMPLIMENT cooking sauces, ORLEANS canned seafood, and AUNT FANNY'S bakery goods, among others.

Just two years ago, we were proud to welcome into the fold the Wm. Underwood Company, the Boston firm that for over 150 years has been producing the kinds of handy, time-saving foods so important to the homemaker — both yesterday and today. High-quality convenience meat spreads, especially the famous UNDERWOOD Deviled Ham, are among our most popular products. And along with its own fine foods, Underwood brought us other respected names and products, including AC'CENT Flavor Enhancer, B&M Baked Beans and Brown Bread, and RICHARDSON & ROBBINS Plum Pudding.

Pet today is a large and diverse family including some of the country's most respected food products — far different from the tiny milk condensing company founded so long ago in the Swiss farming community of Highland, Illinois. But through a century of growth and change, one thing has remained constant — a firm commitment always to provide products distinguished by their convenience and quality.

Time and change have been good to Pet. We not only have kept pace with — but through the years have helped shape — the changing lifestyles of the American consumer.

We knew your parents, your grandparents, perhaps even your great-grandparents. We've met you on grocery shelves with our ever-expanding line of tasty, time-saving food products. We've greeted you at home in magazine, radio, and TV messages sharing important nutritional information and food ideas. We've stood beside you in the kitchen on our product labels and in our recipe books, offering new ways to bring variety and delicious taste to mealtimes. We've been a part of your day from breakfast through midnight snack.

We at Pet are proud that you've made us a part of your family's meal-time traditions. And as we celebrate our 100th birthday, we will continue to bring to your family — your children, your grandchildren, perhaps even your great-grandchildren — products and product information you can trust.

To your family, the best from our family — and thank you.

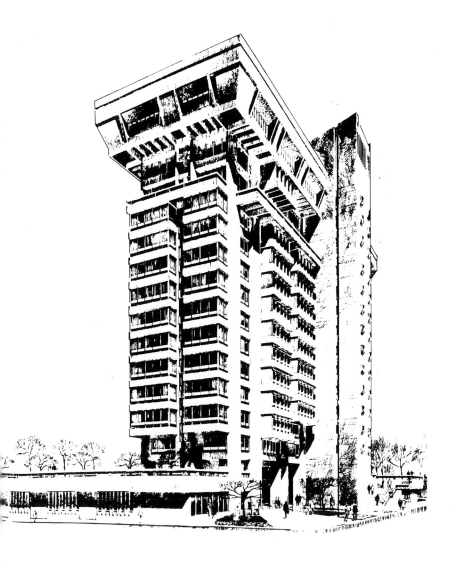

And now ...

We invite you
to join the Kitchens of Pet
in our celebration
of cooking
in America

Let's Get Cooking!

Old-Fashioned Glazed Raisin Bread (page 23), Apple Pie (page 32), Butter Almond Tea Cookies, Double Chocolate Drops (page 15), Peanut Butter Cookies, Chocolate Chip Bars (page 14)

A Sampler of Goodies
From Grandma's Kitchen

14

PEANUT BUTTER COOKIES

6 dozen cookies   *(photograph on page 13)*

1 1/2 **cups all-purpose flour**
1/2 **teaspoon baking powder**
1/2 **teaspoon baking soda**
1/2 **teaspoon salt**
1/2 **teaspoon ground**
   cinnamon
2 1/2 **cups HEARTLAND**
   Natural Cereal, Plain,
   Coconut, or Raisin
1 **cup creamy peanut butter**
1/2 **cup butter or**
   margarine, softened
1/2 **cup firmly packed**
   brown sugar
1/2 **cup granulated sugar**
2 **eggs**
1 **teaspoon vanilla**

Preheat oven to 375°F. Sift together flour, baking powder, baking soda, salt and cinnamon. Stir in HEARTLAND cereal. Cream together peanut butter, butter and sugars. Add eggs, one at a time, beating well after each addition. Stir in vanilla. Gradually add dry ingredients. Form into 1-inch balls. Place on ungreased cookie sheet. Press flat with greased fork to create waffle design. Bake 8 to 10 minutes or until light brown.

CHOCOLATE CHIP BARS

30 cookies   *(photograph on page 13)*

2 1/4 **cups sifted all-purpose**
   flour
1 **teaspoon baking soda**
1/2 **teaspoon salt**
1 **cup butter or margarine,**
   softened
3/4 **cup firmly packed**
   brown sugar
3/4 **cup granulated sugar**
2 **eggs**
1 1/2 **teaspoons vanilla**
1 **cup chopped pecans**
1 **package (12 ounces)**
   WHITMAN'S Semi-Sweet
   Chocolate Chips

Preheat oven to 375°F. Sift together flour, baking soda, and salt. In large bowl, cream butter. Gradually add sugars, beating until light and fluffy. Beat in eggs and vanilla. Gradually add dry ingredients. Stir in pecans and chocolate chips. Spread evenly in greased 15 × 10 × 1-inch jelly-roll pan. Bake 20 to 25 minutes or until golden brown. Let cool. Cut into bars.

BUTTER ALMOND TEA COOKIES

4 to 4½ dozen cookies *(photograph on page 13)*

**2 cups sifted all-purpose
  flour**
¹/₈ teaspoon salt
**¹/₂ cup butter or margarine,
  softened**
**¹/₂ cup firmly packed
  brown sugar**
¹/₂ cup granulated sugar
2 eggs
¹/₂ teaspoon almond extract
¹/₄ cup PET Sour Cream
¹/₂ teaspoon baking soda
¹/₂ cup chopped pecans

Preheat oven to 375°F. Sift together flour and salt. In large bowl, cream butter. Gradually add sugars, beating until light and fluffy. Beat in eggs and almond extract. In separate bowl, mix sour cream and baking soda. Blend half the dry ingredients into butter mixture. Mix in sour cream and then remaining dry ingredients. Stir in pecans. Drop by teaspoonfuls, 2 inches apart, onto greased cookie sheet. Bake for 8 to 10 minutes.

DOUBLE CHOCOLATE DROPS

7 dozen cookies *(photograph on page 13)*

**1 package (12 ounces)
  WHITMAN'S Semi-Sweet
  Chocolate Chips,
  divided usage**
**2 cups sifted all-purpose
  flour**
1 teaspoon baking soda
¹/₂ teaspoon salt
**1 cup butter or margarine,
  softened**
1 cup sugar
2 eggs
2 teaspoons vanilla
¹/₄ cup water
¹/₂ cup chopped nuts

In heavy saucepan or double boiler, melt 1 cup chocolate chips. Let cool. In small bowl, combine flour, baking soda, and salt. In large bowl, cream butter. Gradually add sugar. Beat in eggs and vanilla. Mix in melted chocolate. Blend in half the dry ingredients. Mix in water and then remaining dry ingredients. Stir in nuts and remaining 1 cup chocolate chips. Refrigerate 2 hours. Drop chilled dough by rounded teaspoonfuls, 2 inches apart, onto lightly greased cookie sheets. Bake at 375°F 8 to 10 minutes.

16

OLD-FASHIONED DROP COOKIES

5 dozen cookies

2 cups all-purpose flour
1 1/2 cups firmly packed
    brown sugar
1 teaspoon salt
1/2 teaspoon baking soda
1 cup butter or
    margarine, softened
2 eggs
1 teaspoon vanilla
3 cups HEARTLAND Natural
    Cereal, Plain, Coconut,
    or Raisin
1 cup (6 ounces)
    WHITMAN'S Semi-Sweet
    Chocolate Chips

Preheat oven to 375°F. Stir together flour, brown sugar, salt, and baking soda. Mix in butter, eggs, and vanilla until smooth. Stir in HEARTLAND cereal and chocolate chips. Drop by teaspoonfuls, about 2 inches apart, onto greased cookie sheet. Bake 10 to 12 minutes.

VARIATION: *Cookie batter may be poured into 13 × 9-inch baking pan and baked at 350°F 25 to 30 minutes or until knife inserted 3 inches from edge comes out clean. Cool. Cut into bars.*

OATMEAL CHIPPERS

3 dozen cookies

3/4 cup sifted all-purpose
    flour
1/2 teaspoon baking soda
1/4 teaspoon salt
1/2 cup shortening
1 egg
1/2 teaspoon vanilla
6 tablespoons granulated
    sugar
6 tablespoons firmly packed
    brown sugar
1 cup rolled oats
1 cup (6 ounces)
    WHITMAN'S Semi-Sweet
    Chocolate Chips

Preheat oven to 375°F. In small bowl, combine flour, baking soda, and salt. In large bowl, combine shortening, egg, vanilla, and sugars. Beat until creamy. Blend in flour mixture. Stir in oats and chocolate chips. Drop by teaspoonfuls, 2 inches apart, onto lightly greased cookie sheet. Bake 8 to 10 minutes or until lightly browned.

17

SUGAR COOKIES
4 dozen cookies

**5 cups sifted all-purpose
    flour
3 teaspoons baking powder
1/4 teaspoon salt
1 cup shortening, softened
1 1/2 cups sugar
3 eggs, well beaten
1 teaspoon vanilla
1/2 cup PET Evaporated Milk
    Sugar**

Resift flour with baking powder and salt. Cream together shortening and 1½ cups sugar. Mix in eggs and vanilla. Add half the flour mixture and beat until smooth. Then add evaporated milk and remaining flour mixture; mix well. Refrigerate dough 2 to 3 hours or until firm. Roll dough out to ¼-inch thickness. Cut into shapes and sprinkle with sugar. Bake at 425°F on greased cookie sheet 12 minutes or until light brown.

APPLE NUT LOAF
1 loaf

(photograph on page 207)

**1 1/2 cups all-purpose flour
2 teaspoons baking powder
1/4 teaspoon salt
1/3 cup shortening, softened
1 cup sugar
1 teaspoon vanilla
2 eggs
1 cup chopped unpeeled
    apples
1/2 cup PET Evaporated Milk
1/4 cup chopped walnuts**

Preheat oven to 350°F. In small bowl, stir together flour, baking powder, and salt. In large bowl, cream shortening, sugar, and vanilla; beat until fluffy. Add eggs and beat until well blended. Stir in half the flour mixture. Mix in apples, evaporated milk, and walnuts. Add remaining flour mixture; blend well. Spread batter in greased, 9 × 5-inch loaf pan. Bake 1 hour to 1 hour 10 minutes or until top springs back when lightly touched. Cool 10 minutes and remove from pan. Cool thoroughly on rack.

VARIATION: *Miniature Loaves: Grease 6 miniature loaf pans (approximately 4 × 2 inches) and line bottoms with waxed paper. Prepare batter as directed above. Pour into small pans, filling 2/3 full. Bake at 350°F 35 to 45 minutes or until tops spring back when lightly touched. Remove warm loaves from pans. Peel off waxed paper. Allow to cool.*

Six 4 × 2-inch loaves

FUDGE BROWNIES

16 squares

1 cup all-purpose flour
1/3 cup unsweetened
    cocoa powder
1/2 teaspoon baking powder
1/4 teaspoon salt
1/3 cup shortening, softened
1 cup sugar
1 egg
1/4 cup PET Evaporated Milk
1/2 cup broken walnuts or
    pecans

Preheat oven to 350°F. In small bowl, stir together flour, cocoa, baking powder, and salt. In large bowl, cream shortening, sugar, and egg until light and fluffy. Add evaporated milk. Gradually stir in flour mixture. Stir in nuts. Spread in greased 8-inch square baking pan. Bake 25 to 30 minutes or until top springs back when lightly touched. Cut into squares while warm. Cool in pan.

BLONDE BROWNIES

30 bars

2 cups all-purpose flour
2 teaspoons baking powder
1 1/2 teaspoons salt
2 cups (12 ounces)
    butterscotch morsels
1/2 cup butter or
    margarine
2 cups firmly packed
    brown sugar
4 eggs
1 teaspoon vanilla
2 cups HEARTLAND Natural
    Cereal, Plain

Preheat oven to 350°F. In small bowl, combine flour, baking powder, and salt. In double boiler, melt butterscotch morsels and butter. Remove from heat and stir in brown sugar. Cool 5 minutes. In large mixing bowl, beat butterscotch mixture, eggs, and vanilla. Blend in flour mixture. Stir in HEARTLAND cereal. Spread evenly into greased 15 × 10 × 1-inch jelly-roll pan. Bake 30 minutes or until knife inserted 3 inches from edge comes out clean. Cool. Cut into bars.

PEANUT BUTTER CHEWIES

50 to 60 candy chewies

1 cup corn syrup
2/3 cup sugar
1/2 cup peanut butter
4 cups HEARTLAND Natural
    Cereal, Plain or Raisin

In 3-quart saucepan, combine corn syrup and sugar. Bring to a rolling boil and stir in peanut butter until dissolved. Boil one additional minute. Remove from heat and stir in HEARTLAND cereal. Mix well. Drop by teaspoonfuls onto waxed paper. Let cool.

CHEESECAKE

8 to 10 servings

1 cup graham cracker crumbs
¼ cup butter or margarine, melted
2 packages (8 ounces each) cream cheese, softened
2 eggs
1 cup PET Evaporated Milk
1 cup sugar
1 teaspoon vanilla
½ teaspoon lemon peel
1 can (21 ounces) cherry or peach pie filling

Preheat oven to 350°F. In 8-inch square baking pan, combine graham cracker crumbs and butter. Press mixture into bottom of pan and set aside. In medium mixing bowl, beat cream cheese until fluffy. Add eggs and continue beating until smooth. Gradually add evaporated milk, beating until smooth. Stir in sugar, vanilla, and lemon peel. Pour blended mixture over graham cracker crust and bake 45 minutes until slightly puffed and firm to the touch. Allow cake to cool and then top with pie filling. Chill thoroughly before serving.

CRUNCH BARS

18 bars   *(photograph on page 34)*

4 cups HEARTLAND Natural Cereal, Plain, Coconut, or Raisin
⅓ cup wheat germ
⅓ cup firmly packed brown sugar
¼ cup butter or margarine
3 tablespoons corn syrup

Preheat oven to 350°F. In large bowl, combine HEARTLAND cereal and wheat germ. In 2-quart saucepan over medium heat, cook brown sugar, butter, and corn syrup until brown sugar has melted and mixture is smooth. Pour brown sugar mixture over cereal and mix well. Firmly press into foil-lined 9-inch square baking pan. Bake 12 to 14 minutes or until golden brown. Cool completely. Cut into bars.

The Personal Touch

An early PET Milk salesman was expected also to be an expert window trimmer. Persuading a grocer to display PET Milk in his store window could be the salesman's greatest challenge. Around 1930, Pet's sales department began providing crepe paper banners of orange and blue (PET label colors), posters, large reprints of successful ads, and other window trimmings. The rest was up to the salesman's creative touch.

GRANDMA'S OATMEAL BREAD
Two 8-inch loaves

4 cups all-purpose flour,
    divided usage
¹/₃ cup firmly packed brown
    sugar
1¹/₂ teaspoons salt
2 packages (¹/₄ ounce each)
    active dry yeast
1 cup water
1 tall can (12 fluid ounces)
    PET Evaporated Milk
2 tablespoons shortening
2 cups rolled oats

Step 1: In large mixing bowl, *stir together 1½ cups flour, brown sugar, salt, and yeast.* Heat water, evaporated milk, and shortening until shortening is completely melted. Pour heated mixture over oats.

Step 2: Let oats stand until warm (about 125°F). Add oats to flour mixture and *beat with electric mixer on MEDIUM 2 minutes.* Gradually add enough flour to make a thick batter. Beat batter on HIGH 2 minutes. Mix in remaining flour.

Step 3: Turn dough out onto lightly floured board and *knead until smooth and elastic.*

(continued on page 22)

Grandma's Oatmeal Bread

Step 4: *Place in greased bowl*, cover, and let rise in warm, draft-free place until doubled in bulk. Knead dough down.

Step 5: Divide dough in half. Roll each dough half into 10 × 7-inch rectangle. To form loaves, *roll up each rectangle jelly-roll style* and pinch seam to seal.

Step 6: Fold under ends and *place each loaf seam side down in greased 8 × 4-inch loaf pan.* Cover and let rise in warm, draft-free place until doubled in bulk.

Step 7: When *loaves have doubled*, preheat oven to 375°F. Bake bread 15 minutes. Reduce heat to 350°F and bake an additional 30 to 35 minutes or until bread separates from pan sides.

OLD-FASHIONED GLAZED RAISIN BREAD
2 loaves   *(photograph on page 13)*

**5 cups all-purpose flour,
    divided usage
1 cup seedless raisins
1/2 cup sugar
2 teaspoons salt
1 teaspoon ground cinnamon
2 packages (1/4 ounce each)
    active dry yeast
1 cup PET Evaporated Milk
1 cup water
1/4 cup shortening**

In large mixing bowl, stir together 1½ cups flour, raisins, sugar, salt, cinnamon, and yeast. Over low heat, warm evaporated milk, water, and shortening to 125°F. Add warm milk mixture to flour mixture, and beat with electric mixer on MEDIUM 2 minutes. Gradually add enough flour to form a thick batter. Beat batter on HIGH 2 minutes. By hand, mix in remaining flour; blend well. Turn dough onto lightly floured board, kneading until smooth and elastic. Form dough into smooth ball. Place dough in greased bowl, cover, and let rise in warm, draft-free place until tripled in bulk. Knead down. Shape into 2 loaves and place in 2 greased 8 × 4-inch loaf pans. Again let dough rise until doubled in bulk. Preheat oven to 400°F. Bake bread 15 minutes, then reduce heat to 350°F and bake an additional 30 to 35 minutes. When bread is done, it will shrink away from sides, sound hollow when tapped, and have a dark golden brown crust. Remove warm bread from pan and allow to cool on rack. Glaze cooled loaves.

NOTE: *This bread will develop a rich, deep brown crust when baked.*

CONFECTIONERS GLAZE

**1 1/2 cups sifted
        confectioners sugar
2 tablespoons hot water
1 teaspoon butter or
        margarine, softened**

Combine confectioners sugar, hot water, and butter or margarine; brush over cooled bread.

SPICY APRICOT SNACK CAKE

9 servings

1 cup chopped dried apricots
1 cup water
1 small can (5.33 fluid ounces) PET Evaporated Milk
2 tablespoons lemon juice
1³/₄ cups sifted cake flour
1¹/₂ teaspoons baking powder
1 teaspoon baking soda
¹/₂ teaspoon ground cinnamon
¹/₂ teaspoon ground nutmeg
¹/₄ teaspoon salt
¹/₂ cup butter or margarine, softened
1 cup sugar
1 egg
¹/₂ cup chopped nuts

In small saucepan, combine apricots and water. Bring to a boil over medium heat. Reduce heat, cover, and simmer 15 minutes. Mash cooked apricots to form a pulp, and allow to cool. Preheat oven to 350°F. Stir together evaporated milk and lemon juice. Stir together flour, baking powder, baking soda, cinnamon, nutmeg, and salt. In large bowl, cream butter. Gradually add sugar, and continue to cream until light and fluffy. Beat in egg. Blend in half the dry ingredients. Stir in milk mixture, and then remaining dry ingredients. Stir in apricots and nuts. Pour batter into greased 9-inch square baking pan. Bake 40 to 45 minutes or until toothpick inserted in center comes out clean. Serve snack cake warm or cooled. Sprinkle cooled cake with confectioners sugar.

CINNAMON CRISPS

Approximately 4 dozen crisps

1³/₄ cups sifted all-purpose flour
2 teaspoons baking powder
1 teaspoon ground cinnamon
¹/₂ teaspoon salt
¹/₃ cup shortening
³/₄ cup sugar
¹/₃ cup PET Evaporated Milk
Cinnamon sugar

Preheat oven to 375°F. Stir together flour, baking powder, cinnamon, and salt; set aside. Cream together shortening and sugar. Add half the flour mixture and beat well. Pour in evaporated milk and remaining flour mixture, and mix well. Chill batter 1 hour. Turn out onto floured board. Roll out very thin. Cut into shapes. Sprinkle with cinnamon sugar. Bake on greased cookie sheet 8 to 10 minutes or until light brown.

Play Ball!

That scuffed, dirty baseball *could* look brand new. A former coach at the University of Detroit advocated the use of PET Evaporated Milk as a whitener of battered horsehides. The formula? Pour a little PET on a towel and apply briskly to the ball. Dry it immediately, and the ball, he said, should look like new.

HEARTLAND BREAD

2 loaves   *(photograph on page 211)*

**2 cups HEARTLAND Natural
  Cereal, Plain, Coconut,
  or Raisin**
1 cup hot water
**1 tall can (12 fluid ounces)
  PET Evaporated Milk**
**2 tablespoons butter or
  margarine, softened**
**4 to 5 cups all-purpose
  flour, divided usage**
**1/4 cup firmly packed
  brown sugar**
1 teaspoon salt
**2 packages (1/4 ounce each)
  active dry yeast**

Combine HEARTLAND cereal, hot water, evaporated milk, and butter. Let stand 10 minutes. Stir together 2 cups flour, brown sugar, salt, and yeast. Add cereal mixture. Beat with electric mixer on MEDIUM 2 minutes. Gradually add more flour until a stiff dough forms. Knead on floured board until smooth and elastic. Place in greased bowl. Cover. Let rise in warm, draft-free place about 1 hour or until doubled in bulk. Punch down. Divide dough in half. Form 2 loaves. (To make rolls, see below.) Place in 2 greased 8 × 4-inch loaf pans. Cover and let rise about 1 hour or until doubled in bulk. Preheat oven to 350°F. Bake bread 35 minutes or until loaves sound hollow when tapped. Remove to cooling racks.

VARIATION: HEARTLAND Rolls: *Shape dough into 24 balls. Place on greased cookie sheets. Cover. Let rise until doubled. Bake at 350°F 15 minutes.*

2 dozen rolls

 **HEARTLAND**

In 1972 Pet introduced HEARTLAND Natural Cereals to satisfy the growing appetite for wholesome natural foods.

HEARTLAND'S unique combination of old-fashioned rolled oats, wheat germ and brown sugar — gently toasted to retain the protein and nutrients of the natural grain, and then blended with raisins or coconut — helped attract a whole new group of ready-to-eat cereal lovers. Containing no artificial colors, additives or preservatives, HEARTLAND'S naturally sweet taste and crunchy texture make it good enough to eat straight from the box as a healthy snack, a delicious ice cream topping, or even as a handy ingredient in homemade cookies and candies.

GERMAN CHOCOLATE CAKE
10 to 12 servings

1 cup PET Evaporated Milk
1 tablespoon lemon juice
1 bar (4 ounces) sweet
   cooking chocolate
1 1/2 cups sifted all-purpose
   flour
1 teaspoon baking soda
1/2 teaspoon salt
3/4 cup butter or margarine,
   softened
1 cup sugar
2 eggs
1 teaspoon vanilla
1 cup HEARTLAND Natural
   Cereal, Coconut

Preheat oven to 350°F. Mix evaporated milk and lemon juice; set aside. Melt chocolate in double boiler. Cool slightly. Sift together flour, baking soda, and salt. In large mixing bowl, cream butter. Add sugar. Add eggs and vanilla. Blend in half of dry ingredients. Stir in milk mixture and melted chocolate. Mix in remaining dry ingredients. Stir in HEARTLAND Cereal. Pour into two greased 8-inch round baking pans lined with waxed paper. Bake 30 to 40 minutes or until toothpick inserted in center comes out clean. Cool completely before frosting with Caramel Coconut Frosting.

CARAMEL COCONUT FROSTING
Frosts two 8-inch layers

1 small can (5.33 fluid
   ounces) PET Evaporated
   Milk
1 egg
2/3 cup firmly packed
   brown sugar
1/2 cup butter or margarine,
   softened
1 teaspoon vanilla
1 cup shredded coconut
1/2 cup HEARTLAND Natural
   Cereal, Coconut

In saucepan, heat and stir evaporated milk, egg, brown sugar, and butter until bubbly and thick. Chill until cold and thick. Beat in vanilla and coconut. Frost cooled cake. Sprinkle HEARTLAND Cereal over tops of each layer.

German Chocolate Cake with Caramel Coconut Frosting

Pet's 100 years began with evaporated milk. In fact, our history and the story of evaporated milk — or "Evap," as we at Pet fondly call it — are so closely entwined that the two are almost inseparable. Our first product, Evap was also our sole product for some 35 years.

Today, when fresh milk is available nearly every-where, it's hard to imagine conditions in 1885 when the Helvetia Milk Condensing Company — later to become Pet Incorporated — first introduced canned evaporated milk. Over the next decade the product would become a staple in pantries across America. As a substitute for fresh milk where supplies were scarce or impure, as a rich and creamy ingredient in cooking, and as a convenient, wholesome baby food, Evap truly earned its place in American history.

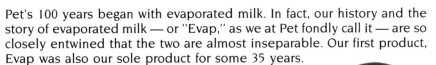

It was John Meyenberg's formula for preserving milk without adding sugar that launched Helvetia, and the labors of early company president Louis Latzer, that kept the new company afloat. Latzer's years of patient, careful research to perfect the canning process led to the first pure milk that could be stored indefinitely without spoilage. The revolutionary product won widespread acclaim, including awards like the gold medal from the 1904 Louisiana Purchase Exposition — the "fair" immortalized in the song, "Meet Me in St. Louis, Louie."

Through the years, the process by which we made our famous product was constantly refined and im-proved. Homogenization created a smoother product, and later, irradia-tion allowed the addition of Vitamin D, the "sunshine vitamin," making our milk well-suited for infant feed-ing. We had always stressed Evap's value for infants; in fact, our very first advertisement for what was then called HIGHLAND Evaporated Cream appeared in *Chaperone Magazine* in 1893 with a headline proclaiming, "It gives health and strength to babies and children."

We've gone through quite a few brand names over the years — from HIGHLAND to ECONOMY, HOME, FIG, SUCCESS, TIN COW, TULIP, and more. But our most pop-ular name was "Our PET," introduced around the turn of the century as a baby-size can that sold for five cents. In time, all other brand names were dropped, and in 1923 we became the Pet Milk Company in recognition of the brand's popularity.

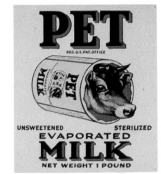

By then, Pet's reputation for consistent quality was well established. Advertising

Happy Hours in Baby Land

based on the "Take Baby and Go" theme was carrying our name across the nation. Our test kitchens and home economists were creating one taste-tempting recipe after another. Mary Lee Taylor was sharing recipe ideas — along with fifteen-minute "true-to-life" dramas — on a radio program that aired on Saturday mornings for over two decades.

Nearly every American housewife had a can of our milk on her kitchen shelf. Homemakers trusted our product's purity and nutritional value and appreciated its economy and convenience. And through the years our name was associated with other names they trusted — spokespersons like Arthur Godfrey, Danny Thomas, Milton Berle, Martha Raye, Red Skelton, and many more.

As fresh milk became widely available, the unique value of our evaporated milk diminished, and we began producing other products with the same fine quality and heritage. By 1966 we had dropped the "Milk" from our name completely, to become Pet Incorporated. But our famous "tin cow" still pops up her head on labels of PET Evap found on kitchen shelves all over the country. PET Evaporated Milk remains a handy, convenient source of milk for family cooking. A shelf-stable product that costs less than cream or half-and-half, it's the milk of choice for adding a rich, creamy taste to cooked dishes. And when holiday time rolls around, and there's pumpkin pie, fudge, or ice cream to be made, it seems nothing else will do.

We've come a long way in a hundred years, and our founders would scarcely recognize their little company today. But that can of evaporated milk has carried us through a long, proud history and, to us, it embodies the Pet philosophy — a dedication to providing convenient, consistently high-quality foods to serve the evolving needs of the American consumer.

PINEAPPLE UPSIDE-DOWN CAKE
10 servings

3 tablespoons butter or margarine
1 cup firmly packed brown sugar
6 slices canned pineapple, drained
Pecan halves
Maraschino cherries, drained
1 1/2 cups all-purpose flour
1 cup granulated sugar
2 teaspoons baking powder
1/2 teaspoon salt
1/2 cup shortening, softened
1/3 cup PET Evaporated Milk
1/4 cup water
1 teaspoon vanilla
2 eggs

Preheat oven to 350°F. In 10-inch ovenproof skillet, melt butter over low heat. Spread brown sugar over butter, coating bottom of skillet evenly. Arrange pineapple slices, pecans and maraschino cherries over brown sugar. In large mixing bowl, stir together flour, granulated sugar, baking powder, and salt. Add shortening, evaporated milk, water, and vanilla. Beat with electric mixer on MEDIUM 2 minutes. Add eggs and beat 2 additional minutes. Pour batter over pineapple slices in skillet. Bake 55 to 60 minutes or until toothpick inserted in center comes out clean. Allow cake to cool 5 minutes before inverting onto serving plate. Serve warm or cold.

Pineapple Upside-Down Cake

FUDGE PECAN PIE

8 servings

¹/₂ cup butter or margarine
3 tablespoons unsweetened
    cocoa powder
³/₄ cup hot water
2 cups sugar
¹/₂ cup all-purpose flour
¹/₈ teaspoon salt
1 small can (5.33 fluid
    ounces) PET Evaporated
    Milk
1 teaspoon vanilla
1 cup pecan halves
1 PET-RITZ Deep Dish
    Pie Crust Shell
1 cup PET WHIP Non-Dairy
    Whipped Topping,
    thawed

Preheat oven and cookie sheet to 350°F. In medium saucepan, melt butter. Add cocoa and stir until dissolved. Add hot water and stir again. With wire whisk, blend in sugar, flour, salt, evaporated milk, and vanilla. Stir until batter is smooth. Mix in pecans and pour into pie crust shell. Bake on preheated cookie sheet 50 minutes or until knife inserted one inch from edge comes out clean. Serve cooled pie with PET WHIP.

APPLE PIE

6 to 8 servings

(photograph on page 13)

2 PET-RITZ Deep Dish
    Pie Crust Shells
4 to 6 tart apples,
    peeled, cored, and
    thinly sliced (5 cups)
2 tablespoons lemon juice
1 cup sugar
2 tablespoons all-purpose
    flour
1 teaspoon ground cinnamon
¹/₈ teaspoon ground nutmeg
2 tablespoons butter or
    margarine

Invert one pie crust shell onto waxed paper, to be used as top crust. Let defrost until flat. In large bowl, sprinkle apples with lemon juice. Preheat oven and cookie sheet to 400°F. Combine 1 cup sugar, flour, cinnamon, and nutmeg. Pour over apples; mix well. Fill bottom pie crust shell with apple mixture. Dot with butter. Fold flattened pie crust in half. Place on top of pie. Unfold and recrimp edges, sealing completely. Cut slits for steam to escape. Sprinkle with sugar. Bake on preheated cookie sheet 40 to 45 minutes or until golden brown. Cool ¹/₂ hour before cutting.

NOTE: *Jonathan apples, which are available throughout the U.S., are excellent baking apples. The apples have a bright red color with a slightly tart, rich flavor.*

PECAN PIE

6 to 8 servings

3 eggs
1 cup sugar
¹/₂ cup corn syrup
¹/₄ cup butter or
　　margarine, melted
1 cup pecan halves
1 PET-RITZ Regular Pie
　　Crust Shell

Preheat oven and cookie sheet to 375°F. Combine eggs, sugar, corn syrup, and melted butter. Beat thoroughly. Stir in pecans. Pour into unbaked pie crust shell. Bake on preheated cookie sheet 30 to 35 minutes or until filling is slightly firm. Center will look soft when pie is gently shaken but will become firm when cooled.

CHOCOLATE PINWHEELS

24 pinwheels

1 cup Creamy Fondant
　　(page 36)
2 teaspoons butter or
　　margarine
¹/₄ cup WHITMAN'S Semi-
　　Sweet Chocolate Chips

Roll fondant out between 2 pieces of waxed paper, creating a ¼-inch thick square. Pull off top piece of waxed paper and trim fondant to create a neat square. Melt butter. Stir in chocolate chips until completely melted. Allow mixture to cool. Spread mixture evenly over fondant to within ¼ inch of edges. Roll up like a jelly roll. Wrap in waxed paper and chill until firm. To serve, let roll stand at room temperature a few minutes and then cut into ¼-inch slices.

As American as Apple Pie

That phrase is highest praise for something with homegrown goodness and country simplicity. Over the years, apple pie in various forms has been eaten by Americans for breakfast, as an entree, and for dessert. In 1758 a Swedish immigrant wrote home about the curious American custom: "Apple pie is used through the whole year and when fresh apples are no longer to be had, dried ones are used. It is the evening meal of children."

HEAVENLY HASH
36 squares of candy

**1 package (12 ounces)
    WHITMAN'S Semi-Sweet
    Chocolate Chips
1 can (14 ounces) sweetened
    condensed milk
1 teaspoon vanilla
4 cups miniature
    marshmallows
1 cup pecan halves
1 cup HEARTLAND Natural
    Cereal, Plain**

Butter bottom and sides of a 9-inch square pan. In large saucepan over medium-low heat, melt chocolate chips. Blend in milk and vanilla, and mix well. Remove from heat. Stir in marshmallows, pecans, and HEARTLAND cereal, mixing until well coated. Pour mixture into buttered pan. Refrigerate until firm, 1½ to 2 hours. Cut candy into small squares. Store in refrigerator.

PEANUT BUTTER FUDGE
18 squares of fudge

**2 cups sugar
¹/₂ cup PET Evaporated Milk
2 tablespoons corn syrup
1 tablespoon lemon juice
¹/₂ cup peanut butter
¹/₂ cup peanuts
1 tablespoon butter or
    margarine
1 teaspoon vanilla**

Butter bottom and sides of 9 × 5-inch loaf pan; set aside. In small saucepan, heat sugar, evaporated milk, corn syrup, and lemon juice to soft ball stage (234°F), stirring constantly. Remove from heat and cool to 225°F. Stir in remaining ingredients and mix well about 2 minutes. Pour into buttered pan. Allow to cool in refrigerator. Store candy in refrigerator.

CHOCOLATE COVERED CHERRY CREAMS
24 candies

**24 maraschino cherries with
    stems, well drained
1 cup Creamy Fondant
    (page 36)
1 cup (6 ounces)
    WHITMAN'S Semi-Sweet
    Chocolate Chips
2 tablespoons paraffin wax,
    melted**

Cover cherries in fondant by shaping 2 teaspoons fondant around each cherry. Leave stems exposed for dipping. In small double boiler, melt chocolate chips and paraffin. Dip fondant-covered cherries into melted chocolate to coat. Place on waxed paper to cool.

*Crunch Bars (page 19), Heavenly Hash, Peanut Butter Fudge,
Chocolate Covered Cherry Creams*

36

CREAMY FONDANT

Approximately 1½ cups

3 tablespoons butter or margarine
¼ teaspoon salt
¼ cup PET Evaporated Milk
1 teaspoon vanilla
4 cups (1 pound) confectioners sugar, sifted

In medium saucepan, melt butter over low heat. Stir in salt, evaporated milk, and vanilla. Remove from heat and gradually add confectioners sugar. Turn mixture onto lightly sugared (confectioners sugar) board. Knead candy until smooth. Fondant can be used as the base of many candies.

CHOCOLATE POPCORN CRUNCH

1½ quarts popcorn crunch

⅔ cup firmly packed brown sugar
½ cup butter or margarine
1 package (12 ounces) WHITMAN'S Semi-Sweet Chocolate Chips
3 cups freshly popped corn
1 cup HEARTLAND Natural Cereal, Plain

In large saucepan, melt brown sugar and butter. Cook, stirring constantly about 5 minutes or until thickened. Add chocolate chips and continue stirring until melted. Stir in popcorn and HEARTLAND cereal. Cook over low heat until all popcorn is well coated. Spread onto greased jelly-roll pan one layer deep. Let cool. Break into pieces.

NOTE: *This may be stored in refrigerator several days.*

Saturday Night Supper (page 41), Chicken Divan Roll-Ups (page 38), Shrimp Chili Quiche (page 50)

The Family Gathers

CHICKEN DIVAN ROLL-UPS

5 servings, 2 roll-ups per serving   *(photograph on page 37)*

1 package (10 ounces) flaky buttermilk biscuits
2 cans (4³/₄ ounces each) UNDERWOOD Chunky Chicken Spread
1 package (10 ounces) frozen broccoli spears, prepared according to package directions
1 cup (4 ounces) shredded process American cheese
³/₄ cup PET Evaporated Milk

Preheat oven to 375°F. On floured surface, roll out each biscuit into 4 × 3-inch oval. Spread scant 2 tablespoons chicken spread over center of each biscuit. Arrange 2 broccoli spears on each biscuit so flower ends extend beyond edge of roll. Fold ends of dough over broccoli so they overlap; pinch to seal. Place biscuits on ungreased cookie sheet and bake 15 minutes or until golden brown. Meanwhile, in heavy saucepan, combine cheese and evaporated milk. Stir mixture over low heat until cheese is completely melted. Serve sauce over biscuits.

CHICKEN AND BROCCOLI AU GRATIN

6 servings

¹/₄ cup butter or margarine
¹/₄ cup chopped onion
¹/₄ cup all-purpose flour
1 teaspoon salt
¹/₂ teaspoon curry powder
Dash black pepper
1 can (4 ounces) sliced mushrooms
1 tall can (12 fluid ounces) PET Evaporated Milk
1 package (10 ounces) frozen broccoli spears, cooked and drained
1 chicken (2 to 2¹/₂ pounds), cooked and cut into large cubes
1 cup (4 ounces) shredded Monterey Jack cheese

Preheat oven to 375°F. In skillet, melt butter. Sauté onion until transparent. Remove from heat. Stir in flour, salt, curry powder, and pepper. Drain mushrooms, reserving liquid. If needed, add enough water to make ½ cup liquid and gradually stir into flour mixture in skillet. Blend in evaporated milk until smooth. Add mushrooms. Return to heat. Cook and stir over medium heat until sauce begins to thicken. Arrange broccoli spears and chicken on bottom of 13 × 9-inch baking dish. Pour sauce over. Top with cheese. Bake 20 minutes or until bubbly around edges. Cool 15 minutes before serving.

39

CHICKEN IN RED SESAME SAUCE

6 servings

¼ **cup toasted sesame seeds**
¼ **teaspoon cayenne pepper**
6 **chicken legs with thighs attached (3 pounds)**
¼ **cup lard or vegetable oil**
1 **large onion, finely chopped**
2 **garlic cloves, minced**
2 **cans (10 ounces each) OLD EL PASO Tomatoes and Green Chilies**
1 **can (4 ounces) OLD EL PASO Chopped Green Chilies**
1 **tablespoon cornstarch**
1 **tablespoon chili powder**
1 **teaspoon salt**
½ **teaspoon ground cinnamon**
½ **teaspoon ground coriander**
¼ **teaspoon ground cloves**
¼ **teaspoon crushed anise seed**
  Salt and freshly ground black pepper to taste
  Hot cooked rice (optional)

Combine sesame seed and cayenne pepper. In large skillet, brown chicken legs on all sides in hot lard or vegetable oil. Spoon off fat. Add onion, garlic, tomatoes and green chilies, green chilies, cornstarch, chili powder, salt, cinnamon, coriander, cloves, anise seed, and sesame seed mixture. Bring to a boil; cover and reduce heat. Simmer 1 hour or until chicken is tender. Remove chicken from sauce. Bring sauce to a boil and cook, stirring frequently, until sauce is reduced and thickened. Add salt and pepper. Serve with rice if desired.

To toast sesame seeds: *Spread in shallow pan; bake in preheated 350°F oven, stirring occasionally, 5 to 7 minutes or until golden brown.*

Part of the Team

When peaks are conquered and history made, Underwood often plays a "sustaining" role. UNDERWOOD canned goods first set sail for adventure in 1838 with six Naval ships on an exploring expedition to the South Seas. Over a century later, good-tasting, energy-packed UNDERWOOD spreads and sardines nourished two American women as they made mountain climbing history by struggling to the summit of Nepal's 26,504-foot-high Annapurna I. And in 1963, UNDERWOOD meat spreads sustained the first U.S. climbers to conquer Mount Everest. "Particularly at the very highest elevations when cooking was almost impossible," said the team's leader, "these spreads really proved their worth."

PERFECT PORK AND CHICKEN PIE

6 servings

2 PET-RITZ Deep Dish Pie Crust Shells
8 ounces pork sausage
1/4 cup butter or margarine
1/3 cup all-purpose flour
1 teaspoon celery seeds
1/2 teaspoon paprika
1/2 teaspoon poultry seasoning
1/4 teaspoon curry powder
1/4 teaspoon salt
1/8 teaspoon freshly ground black pepper
1 can (13 1/2 ounces) chicken broth
2/3 cup milk
2 cups cubed cooked chicken
1 package (10 ounces) frozen peas, thawed

Invert one pie crust shell onto waxed paper. Let defrost until flat. Preheat oven and cookie sheet to 375°F. In large skillet, brown sausage. Drain well on paper towels. In same skillet, melt butter. Blend in flour, celery seed, paprika, poultry seasoning, curry powder, salt, and pepper. Stir in chicken broth and milk. Cook and stir until thick and bubbly. Cook 1 additional minute. Add chicken, sausage, and peas. Pour into pie crust. Cover with flattened crust. Seal edge. Cut slits for steam to escape. Bake on preheated cookie sheet 45 to 50 minutes or until golden brown.

SATURDAY NIGHT SUPPER

4 servings   *(photograph on page 37)*

4 center cut pork chops, thinly sliced
1 tablespoon vegetable oil
1 can (28 ounces) B&M Brick Oven Baked Beans
2 tablespoons apple jelly
2 teaspoons water
8 slices apple
Ground cinnamon

Preheat oven to 350°F. In skillet, brown chops evenly in hot oil, about 10 minutes on each side. Drain chops on paper towels. Pour beans into 2-quart casserole and place chops on top of beans. Bake 45 minutes. In small bowl, combine jelly and water. Baste chops with jelly mixture and arrange apple slices on top. Sprinkle with cinnamon. Return to oven and continue baking an additional 15 minutes.

Perfect Pork and Chicken Pie

SPARERIBS COUNTRY STYLE

6 servings

6 pounds (2 racks) spareribs, cut into serving pieces
2 teaspoons AC'CENT Flavor Enhancer
1 1/2 teaspoons salt
2 lemons, thinly sliced
1/2 cup prepared mustard
1/2 cup vinegar
1/2 cup catsup
1/4 cup Worcestershire sauce
2 teaspoons chili powder

Preheat oven to 350°F. Line 2 large shallow baking pans with aluminum foil. Place spareribs in pans, meaty side up. Sprinkle with AC'CENT and salt; top with lemon slices. Bake 1 hour. Pour off fat; refrigerate spareribs until ready to grill. To prepare sauce, in small bowl combine mustard, vinegar, catsup, Worcestershire sauce, and chili powder. Place spareribs on aluminum foil-lined grill, 6 to 8 inches from heat. Brush with sauce. Grill 10 to 15 minutes, turning and basting frequently with sauce.

BEEF BIRDS

5 or 6 beef birds

(photograph on page 211)

2 pounds beef round steak or sirloin steak, cut into 5 or 6 portions
1/2 cup chopped dill pickle
1 can (4 ounces) OLD EL PASO Chopped Green Chilies
2 tablespoons chopped green onion
3 slices bacon, fried crisp, drained, and crumbled
Vegetable oil
1 cup beef broth
Salt and freshly ground black pepper to taste

Preheat oven to 325°F. Flatten steak portions with meat mallet to 1/8-inch thickness. Combine pickle, green chilies, green onion, and bacon. Place 2 to 3 tablespoons pickle mixture on each piece of steak. Roll meat jelly-roll fashion. Secure with toothpicks. Brown in one inch of hot oil; drain. Place in 8-inch square baking dish. Pour beef broth over, cover, and bake 1 hour or until meat is tender. Sprinkle with salt and pepper.

STUFFED FLANK STEAK

4 to 6 servings

1 to 1 1/2 pounds beef
    flank steak
1/4 cup vinegar
1 teaspoon salt
1/2 teaspoon freshly ground
    black pepper
2 eggs
1 can (4 ounces) OLD EL PASO
    Whole Green Chilies,
    cut into strips
2 tablespoons chopped
    pimientos
2 tablespoons vegetable oil
1 tablespoon chopped onion
1 small garlic clove, minced
2 tablespoons all-purpose
    flour
1 teaspoon chili powder
2 cups beef broth
    Chopped fresh parsley

Open steak by splitting it to form 2 "pages," leaving a hinge to form a single extended steak that covers twice the area of the original; cut with the grain of the meat. Season meat with vinegar, salt, and pepper. Beat eggs and cook in small skillet until set. Cut into strips. Arrange strips of eggs and chilies alternately over extended meat, parallel to the grain. Sprinkle with chopped pimientos. Roll meat so grain runs the length of the roll, and tie securely in several places with string. In skillet, heat oil and fry rolled meat on all sides until brown. Place in baking pan. Preheat oven to 350°F. Add onion and garlic to drippings in skillet and cook a few minutes. Add flour and chili powder; cook 2 minutes. Add broth and mix well. Cook over low heat 5 minutes to thicken. Pour sauce over rolled meat and bake, basting occasionally, 1 hour for medium rare, or 1½ hours for well-done. Top with chopped parsley.

FLUFFY MASHED POTATOES

4 servings   *(photograph on page 211)*

4 medium potatoes, peeled
    and quartered (about
    1 1/2 pounds)
3/4 cup PET Evaporated Milk
1 teaspoon salt
    Dash black pepper

Place potatoes in saucepan and cover with water. Bring water to a boil, cover, and cook potatoes about 20 minutes or until tender. Drain potatoes and mash. Add evaporated milk, salt, and pepper; beat mixture until light and fluffy. For softer mashed potatoes, additional evaporated milk may be added as desired.

Stuffed Flank Steak

CHEESY RICE BAKE

Six ¾-cup servings

2½ cups water
**1 cup uncooked long
    grain rice**
1 chicken bouillon cube
**1 can (10¾ ounces) cream
    of chicken soup**
**1½ cups (6 ounces) cubed
    process American cheese**
**1 small can (5.33 fluid
    ounces) PET Evaporated
    Milk**
¼ cup chopped pimientos
½ teaspoon salt
    Paprika

Heat water, rice, and bouillon cube to a boil. Stir to dissolve cube. Cover and cook over low heat 20 to 25 minutes or until rice is tender. Remove cover. Continue to cook 4 to 5 minutes or until rice is dry and fluffy. Add soup, cheese, evaporated milk, pimientos, and salt, and mix well. Pour into greased 1½-quart baking dish. Sprinkle with paprika. Bake at 350°F 25 to 35 minutes or until bubbly.

CHEDDAR BAKED BEANS

6 servings

**1 can (28 ounces) B&M
    Brick Oven Baked Beans**
6 slices tomato
**6 cubes Cheddar cheese
    (1½-inch squares)**
    Small raw onion rings
**2 tablespoons red pepper
    relish**

Preheat oven to 375°F. Pour beans into 2-quart casserole. Heat 20 minutes or until bubbly. Remove from oven and top with tomato slices and then cheese cubes. Return to oven and heat 5 to 7 minutes or until cheese is melted. Garnish with onion rings filled with red pepper relish.

CHEESY POTATOES

6 servings

6 medium potatoes
2 tablespoons butter
**1 can (11.1 ounces)
    COMPLIMENT Meat Loaf
    Cooking Sauce**
**1 cup (4 ounces) shredded
    Mozzarella cheese**
    Paprika

Peel potatoes and cut into large cubes. Melt butter in large skillet and add potatoes. Stir in COMPLIMENT and heat until sauce boils. Cover, lower heat, and cook 45 minutes or until potatoes are tender, stirring occasionally. When potatoes are tender, remove from heat and gently stir in cheese. Serve hot, garnished with paprika.

FIESTA CHEESE BAKE

8 to 10 servings

10 eggs
1/2 cup all-purpose flour
1 tablespoon baking powder
1/4 teaspoon salt
1/2 cup butter or margarine,
 melted
1 pint PET Cottage Cheese
4 cups (1 pound) shredded
 Monterey Jack cheese
2 cans (4 ounces each)
 OLD EL PASO Chopped
 Green Chilies
OLD EL PASO Taco Sauce
 or OLD EL PASO Picante
 Salsa (optional)

Preheat oven to 400°F. In large mixing bowl, beat eggs until fluffy. Add flour, baking powder, salt, and melted butter; beat mixture until well blended. Stir in cottage cheese, Monterey Jack cheese, and green chilies. Pour mixture into greased 13 × 9-inch baking pan. Bake 15 minutes. Reduce heat to 350°F and bake an additional 30 to 35 minutes or until golden brown. Cool slightly before cutting. Serve with taco sauce or picante salsa if desired.

DAIRY

Thanks to their mild winters and generous rainfall, America's southern states are especially suited for dairy farming. Pet's Dairy Division got its start in the mountains of eastern Tennessee, with the purchase of a fluid-milk processing plant in Johnson City in 1929. Shortly thereafter, an ice cream plant was purchased in nearby Greeneville, enabling us to turn excess fresh cream into ice cream.

The following half-century brought change and growth. As the popularity of our products grew, we built many dairies and bought others. Dry-ice refrigeration and then refrigerated trucks let us bring our fresh milk and milk products and ice cream to a wider market.

Our high-quality dairy foods won us friends and loyal customers throughout the South. Today, those customers associate the PET name with favorites such as fresh milk, cottage cheese, yogurt, new brands such as Great Ice Creams of the South and Cellini ice cream, and even refrigerated products such as orange juice and fruit drinks.

CAULIFLOWER WITH MUSHROOM CHEESE SAUCE

6 servings

1 **medium head cauliflower**
1 1/2 **cups sliced fresh mushrooms**
2 **tablespoons butter or margarine, melted**
1 **tablespoon all-purpose flour**
1/4 **teaspoon salt**
Dash white pepper
1 **cup PET Evaporated Milk**
1 **cup (4 ounces) shredded sharp process American cheese**
1 **teaspoon prepared mustard**
1 **tablespoon snipped parsley**

Rinse and remove leaves from cauliflower. Place whole head in small amount of boiling salted water. Cover and cook 15 minutes or just until tender. Drain thoroughly. Keep warm. Meanwhile, sauté mushrooms in butter until tender. Blend in flour, salt, and white pepper. Add evaporated milk all at once. Cook over low heat, stirring constantly, until thickened. Stir in cheese and mustard. Heat until cheese melts. Place warm cauliflower on serving platter. Pour cheese sauce over cauliflower. Sprinkle with parsley.

TUNA RICE CASSEROLE

4 to 6 servings

2/3 **cup uncooked instant rice**
1 **can (6 1/2 ounces) tuna, drained**
2 **tablespoons sliced pimiento-stuffed olives**
1 **tall can (12 fluid ounces) PET Evaporated milk**
1 **can (11 ounces) Cheddar cheese soup**
1 **tablespoon parsley flakes**
2 **teaspoons minced onion**
1 **teaspoon dry mustard**
1/2 **teaspoon salt**
Dash black pepper
1/2 **cup (2 ounces) shredded Cheddar cheese**

Preheat oven to 350°F. Place rice in bottom of greased 1 1/2-quart casserole and cover with tuna. Sprinkle with olives. In large mixing bowl, blend evaporated milk, soup, parsley flakes, onion, mustard, salt, and pepper. Pour mixture over tuna and top with cheese. Bake 30 minutes or until bubbly.

Cauliflower with Mushroom Cheese Sauce

SHRIMP CHILI QUICHE

6 servings

(photograph on page 37)

1 can (4¹/4 ounces) ORLEANS
    Deveined Medium
    Shrimp, drained
2 eggs
1 small can (5.33 fluid
    ounces) PET Evaporated
    Milk
2 tablespoons all-purpose
    flour
³/4 teaspoon garlic salt
¹/2 cup (2 ounces) shredded
    Cheddar cheese
¹/2 cup (2 ounces) shredded
    Monterey Jack cheese
¹/2 cup chopped onions
1 can (4 ounces) OLD EL PASO
    Chopped Green Chilies
1 PET-RITZ Regular Pie
    Crust Shell

Preheat oven and cookie sheet to 350°F. Rinse shrimp under cold running water. Drain. Beat together eggs, evaporated milk, flour, and garlic salt (mixture need not be smooth). Stir in cheeses, onions, and green chilies. Pour into pie shell. Place shrimp on top of custard mixture. Bake on preheated cookie sheet 35 to 40 minutes or until knife inserted in center comes out clean. Cool 10 minutes before serving.

SALMON QUICHE

6 servings

1 can (8 ounces) salmon,
    drained
1 small can (5.33 fluid
    ounces) PET Evaporated
    Milk
1 cup (4 ounces) shredded
    Cheddar cheese
¹/2 cup diced onions
2 eggs, separated
1 tablespoon parsley flakes
1 tablespoon lemon juice
1 teaspoon seasoned salt
¹/4 teaspoon freshly ground
    black pepper
1 PET-RITZ Regular Pie
    Crust Shell

Preheat oven and cookie sheet to 375°F. Remove bone and skin from salmon. Flake salmon and mix with evaporated milk, cheese, onions, egg yolks, parsley flakes, lemon juice, seasoned salt, and pepper. Beat egg whites until stiff peaks form. Fold egg whites into salmon mixture. Spoon into pie shell. Bake on preheated cookie sheet 30 to 35 minutes or until filling puffs up and is golden brown. Cool 10 minutes before serving.

SHRIMP AU GRATIN

4 servings

**2 cans (4¼ ounces each)
    ORLEANS Deveined
    Medium or Large Shrimp**
**6 tablespoons butter or
    margarine**
**5 tablespoons all-purpose
    flour**
½ teaspoon salt
**1 tall can (12 fluid ounces)
    PET Evaporated Milk**
½ cup water
**½ cup (2 ounces) shredded
    Swiss cheese**
**½ cup (2 ounces) grated
    Parmesan cheese**
**1 to 2 tablespoons brandy
    (optional)**

Preheat oven to 400°F. Rinse shrimp under cold running water. Drain. In medium saucepan, melt butter. Remove pan from heat. Stir in flour and salt to make a smooth paste. Gradually add evaporated milk and water, stirring constantly. Add cheeses. Return to medium-low heat. Stirring constantly, cook until cheese melts and sauce starts to thicken. Gently stir in shrimp and brandy if desired. Pour into buttered 2-quart baking dish. Bake 20 minutes or until light brown on top.

BROCCOLI CASSEROLE

8 servings

**2 packages (10 ounces each)
    frozen broccoli spears**
**1 can (10¾ ounces) cream of
    mushroom soup**
**1 small can (5.33 fluid
    ounces) PET Evaporated
    Milk**
**1 cup (4 ounces) shredded
    Cheddar cheese**
**1 can (2.8 ounces) French
    fried onion rings**

Preheat oven to 350°F. Prepare broccoli according to package directions, using minimum cooking time. Drain broccoli and arrange evenly over bottom of 2-quart baking dish. In small mixing bowl, blend soup and evaporated milk. Pour mixture over broccoli and top with cheese. Bake 25 minutes. Remove casserole from oven, top with onion rings, and bake an additional 8 to 10 minutes.

QUICHE AMERICANA
6 servings

8 hot dogs, thinly sliced
1 medium onion, sliced
2 tablespoons butter or margarine, melted
1 1/2 cups (6 ounces) cubed process American cheese (1/4-inch cubes), divided usage
1 PET-RITZ Deep Dish Pie Crust Shell
4 eggs
1 tablespoon all-purpose flour
1/4 teaspoon allspice
1/4 teaspoon dry mustard
1/8 teaspoon freshly ground black pepper
2/3 cup milk
Paprika

Preheat oven and cookie sheet to 400°F. In large skillet, brown hot dog slices and onion in butter. Sprinkle half the cheese on bottom of pie crust shell. Cover with hot dog mixture. In small bowl, mix eggs, flour, allspice, mustard, and pepper until well blended. Stir in milk. Pour over hot dogs. Cover with remaining cheese. Sprinkle with paprika. Bake on preheated cookie sheet 15 minutes; reduce oven temperature to 325°F and bake 25 to 30 minutes or until golden brown. Cool 10 minutes before serving.

SPAGHETTI CASSEROLE
6 servings

1 cup broken spaghetti
2 tablespoons vegetable oil
1/2 cup canned or fresh chopped mushrooms
1/4 cup chopped onion
1/4 cup chopped green pepper
1 garlic clove, minced
1/2 cup strained tomatoes or tomato juice
1/4 cup PET Evaporated Milk
1/2 teaspoon salt
1/2 teaspoon oregano
1/2 bay leaf, crushed
1/2 cup (2 ounces) shredded process American cheese
2 tablespoons sliced olives (optional)
Parmesan cheese to taste

Preheat oven to 300°F. Cook spaghetti according to package directions. Drain and rinse with cold water. In saucepan, heat oil. Add mushrooms, onion, green pepper, and garlic. Cook vegetables until tender. Remove from heat and add tomatoes, evaporated milk, salt, oregano, and bay leaf. Combine spaghetti, tomato mixture, American cheese, and olives if desired. Pour into 1 1/2-quart baking dish. Sprinkle with Parmesan cheese. Bake 30 to 35 minutes or until slightly firm.

53

ASPARAGUS-TUNA NOODLE CASSEROLE
Six 1-cup servings

1 **pound fresh asparagus**
   or 1 package (10 ounces)
   frozen asparagus cuts
   and tips
1/2 **cup boiling water**
3 **tablespoons butter or**
   margarine
3 **tablespoons all-purpose**
   flour
1 1/2 **teaspoons salt**
1/2 **teaspoon dry mustard**
1 1/2 **teaspoons Worcestershire**
   sauce
1 **tall can (12 ounces)**
   PET Evaporated Milk
1 **can (6 1/2 ounces) tuna,**
   drained
3 **cups cooked shell noodles**
3/4 **cup sliced ripe olives**
2 **cups (8 ounces) grated**
   Cheddar cheese,
   divided usage

Preheat oven to 350°F. Clean and cut fresh asparagus into 1- to 2-inch pieces. In large saucepan, cook asparagus in boiling water until tender. Stir in butter. Set aside. In small mixing bowl, combine flour, salt, mustard, and Worcestershire sauce. Gradually stir in evaporated milk. Mix until smooth. Pour milk mixture over asparagus. Cook and stir until mixture thickens. Stir in tuna, noodles, olives, and 1 cup cheese. Pour into shallow greased 2-quart baking dish. Sprinkle remaining 1 cup cheese over top. Bake 20 to 25 minutes or until hot and bubbly. Serve hot.

GARDEN EGGPLANT
Eight 1/2-cup servings

1/4 **cup butter or margarine**
2 **medium onions, sliced**
1 **cup sliced celery**
2 **medium eggplant,**
   peeled and cut into
   1-inch cubes
1 **cup chopped green**
   peppers
2 **tablespoons all-purpose**
   flour
2 **teaspoons paprika**
1 1/2 **teaspoons salt**
1 **small can (5.33 fluid**
   ounces) PET Evaporated
   Milk

In large saucepan, melt butter. Stir in onions and celery. Cook over medium heat until onions are translucent. Stir in eggplant and green peppers. Cover. Cook over medium heat 10 to 15 minutes, stirring occasionally, until eggplant is tender. Combine flour, paprika, and salt. Sprinkle over vegetables. Gently stir in evaporated milk. Heat to steaming. Serve hot.

BEAN AND HAM ROLL-UPS

6 servings

**1 can (28 ounces) B&M
    Brick Oven Baked Beans
12 slices baked or
    boiled ham
2 tablespoons butter or
    margarine
¹/₄ cup firmly packed
    brown sugar
1 ¹/₂ tablespoons prepared
    mustard**

Preheat oven to 350°F. Spoon beans in strip at narrow ends of ham slices. Roll up ham slices beginning at narrow end so that beans are enclosed in roll. Arrange ham rolls in shallow baking dish. In small saucepan, melt butter. Add brown sugar and mustard. Cook over low heat, stirring until well blended. Baste tops of rolls with mustard glaze. Bake about 25 minutes, basting occasionally. Garnish with green pepper slices if desired.

GLAZED CARROTS

6 to 8 servings

(photograph on page 211)

**¹/₃ cup butter or margarine
¹/₂ cup water
4 teaspoons sugar
2 to 3 pounds mini-carrots
    (3 to 4 inches long),
    or standard size carrots
    cut into julienne strips
1 teaspoon AC'CENT Flavor
    Enhancer
¹/₂ teaspoon salt
    Freshly ground black
    pepper to taste
    Fresh parsley (optional)**

In medium skillet, melt butter, and add water and sugar. Add carrots; cover and simmer until carrots are tender, adding water as necessary to prevent sticking. Remove cover and bring to a boil. Cook and stir until all liquid has evaporated and carrots are glazed, stirring gently. Sprinkle with AC'CENT, salt, and pepper. Garnish with parsley if desired.

SPECIAL SPINACH QUICHE
6 servings

3 tablespoons chopped onion
2 tablespoons butter or
    margarine
1 package (10 ounces) frozen
    chopped spinach,
    cooked and drained
1 cup (4 ounces) shredded
    Swiss cheese
¹/₃ cup grated Parmesan
    cheese
1 tablespoon all-purpose flour
1 PET-RITZ Deep Dish Pie
    Crust Shell
1 ¹/₂ cups PET Light Cream
3 eggs, slightly beaten
1 teaspoon salt
¹/₂ teaspoon white pepper
¹/₄ teaspoon marjoram
¹/₄ teaspoon basil
¹/₂ teaspoon Worcestershire
    sauce
¹/₈ teaspoon ground nutmeg
    (optional)

Preheat oven and cookie sheet to 375°F. In medium skillet, sauté onion in butter until translucent. Remove from heat. Stir in spinach, Swiss cheese, Parmesan cheese, and flour. Place in bottom of pie crust shell. In small bowl, combine cream, eggs, salt, pepper, marjoram, basil, Worcestershire sauce, and nutmeg if desired. Blend well. Pour over spinach mixture. Bake on preheated cookie sheet 40 to 45 minutes or until knife inserted in center comes out clean. Cool 10 minutes before serving.

Sour Cream Biscuits (page 76), Creamy Scrambled Eggs (page 58), Aloha Treat (page 72), DOWNYFLAKE Pancakes, Bakery Products from PET Bakery Division

It's a New Day

CREAMY SCRAMBLED EGGS

3 servings   *(photograph on page 57)*

6 **eggs**
$^1/_2$ **cup PET Evaporated Milk**
$^1/_2$ **teaspoon salt**
  Dash black pepper
2 **tablespoons butter or
    margarine**

Beat together eggs, evaporated milk, salt, and pepper until well blended. In 10-inch skillet, melt butter. Pour egg mixture into hot skillet and cook over low heat, gently stirring eggs occasionally until cooked to desired firmness.

NOTE: *The secret to fluffy, tender scrambled eggs is cooking over low heat and gently lifting and turning set egg mixture. Much stirring will cause fluffy eggs to break down.*

SICILIAN STYLE QUICHE

6 servings as main dish
10 to 12 servings as appetizer

1 **PET-RITZ Deep Dish
    Pie Crust Shell**
$^1/_2$ **pound bacon, fried
    crisp and drained**
1 **cup (4 ounces) shredded
    Swiss cheese**
2 **eggs, slightly beaten**
$^3/_4$ **cup PET Sour Cream**
2 **tablespoons chopped
    parsley**

Remove frozen pie crust shell from aluminum pie plate. Place crust in 9-inch round cake pan. Let crust thaw. When crust begins to conform to shape of cake pan, gently press to mold to pan. Preheat oven and cookie sheet to 425°F. Crumble cooked bacon over pie shell; top with cheese. Mix eggs, sour cream, and parsley. Pour over cheese. Bake on preheated cookie sheet 20 to 25 minutes or until cheese puffs up and is lightly browned. Cool 10 minutes before serving.

Littlest Customers

Triplets and quadruplets are usually small and are often premature. Such babies must be fed carefully. In the 1930s and '40s, PET Evaporated Milk was a popular infant food, and Pet did its part to help bewildered parents cope with a sudden population explosion. Beginning with the tiny Kasper quads born in 1936 in Passaic, New Jersey, Pet "adopted" 10 sets of quads, setting up trust funds to pay for clothing, housing, and medical care. Of course, they and more than 1,400 sets of triplets were provided a constant supply of PET Milk.

HAM 'N' SWISS IN A SHELL

6 servings   *(photograph on page 207)*

1 **package (10 ounces)**
   frozen spinach
1 **cup chopped cooked ham**
1 **PET-RITZ Deep Dish Pie**
   Crust Shell
1 1/2 **cups (6 ounces) shredded**
   Swiss cheese
4 **eggs**
1 **cup milk**
1/2 **teaspoon basil**
1/4 **teaspoon garlic powder**
1/4 **teaspoon freshly ground**
   black pepper
1/8 **teaspoon salt**

Preheat oven and cookie sheet to 350°F. Prepare spinach according to package directions. Drain well. Sprinkle ham over pie crust. Arrange spinach over ham. Sprinkle with cheese. Stir eggs, milk, basil, garlic powder, pepper, and salt until mixed but not frothy. Pour over cheese. Bake on preheated cookie sheet 30 to 35 minutes or until knife inserted in center comes out clean. Cool 10 minutes before serving.

VARIATION: *Ham 'n' Swiss Company Style: To serve at a buffet, you may prepare this quiche in a 15 × 10 × 1-inch jelly-roll pan. Cut two 20-inch-long strips of waxed paper. Place waxed paper on dampened counter, overlapping lengthwise. Moisture should hold the paper securely. Remove 4 PET-RITZ Deep Dish Pie Crust Shells from freezer. Invert onto waxed paper and remove aluminum foil pans. Cover tops of crusts with two more 20-inch-long strips of waxed paper. Let crusts thaw at room temperature 10 to 15 minutes or until all crusts are flattened. While crusts are thawing, prepare a double recipe of filling. Preheat oven to 400°F. Roll thawed crusts out to form a large rectangle (about 18½ × 13½ inches). Carefully remove top sheets of waxed paper. Ease pastry loosely into pan, with bottom paper now on top. Carefully remove waxed paper. Trim pastry ½ inch from edge of pan. Fold excess pastry under and form edge. Prick bottoms and sides of crust. Partially bake crust 8 to 10 minutes. Remove crust from oven and allow to cool. Reduce oven temperature to 350°F. Fill cooled crust with filling. Bake 40 to 50 minutes or until knife inserted one inch from edge comes out clean. Let stand 10 minutes before slicing.*

15 servings

QUICHE LORRAINE
6 servings

**6 slices bacon, cooked crisp
    and crumbled**
**1 can (4 ounces) sliced
    mushrooms, drained**
**1 cup (4 ounces) shredded
    Swiss cheese**
½ cup diced onion
1 tablespoon all-purpose flour
½ teaspoon salt
¼ teaspoon garlic powder
**1 PET-RITZ Regular Pie Crust
    Shell**
2 eggs
**1 small can (5.33 fluid ounces)
    PET Evaporated Milk**

Preheat oven and cookie sheet to 325°F. In bowl, combine bacon, mushrooms, cheese, onion, flour, salt, and garlic powder. Mix until well blended. Spoon into pie crust. Beat together eggs and evaporated milk. Slowly pour over bacon mixture. Bake on preheated cookie sheet 55 to 60 minutes or until knife inserted in center comes out clean. Cool 10 minutes before serving.

Mini Quiche Lorraine

VARIATION: Mini Quiche Lorraine:

Step 1: Invert 2 PET-RITZ Deep Pie Crust Shells onto waxed paper and remove aluminum foil pans. Cover each crust with another piece of waxed paper. Allow crust to thaw at room temperature until flattened. Preheat oven and cookie sheet to 325°F.

Step 2: Roll out crusts to get flat, smooth surface. Remove top sheets of waxed paper. Cut 6 small circles of pastry (3 from each crust) to fit miniature pie pans. Ease pastry into pans. If necessary, trim crusts, leaving enough pastry to form edge.

(continued on page 62)

62

Step 3: Mix bacon, mushrooms, cheese, onion, flour, salt, and garlic powder. Fill crusts. Beat together eggs and evaporated milk. *Pour over bacon mixture.* Bake on cookie sheet 30 to 35 minutes or until knife inserted one inch from edge comes out clean. Cool 5 minutes before serving.

GOOD MORNING CASSEROLE

12 servings

4 slices bread, quartered
5 eggs, beaten
1 tall can (12 fluid ounces)
   PET Evaporated Milk
1 cup water
2 cups (8 ounces) shredded
   Cheddar cheese
1 pound sausage, cut
   into pieces, browned,
   and drained
1 1/2 teaspoons dry mustard
1 teaspoon salt

Line bottom of 13 × 9-inch baking pan with bread pieces. In large mixing bowl, combine remaining ingredients. Pour over bread and refrigerate 4 to 5 hours or overnight. Bake at 350°F 35 to 45 minutes or until golden brown.

63

HUEVOS RANCHEROS

6 servings

**6 OLD EL PASO Corn
   Tortillas
   Oil for frying
1/2 cup chopped onions
1 garlic clove, minced
2 tablespoons vegetable oil
1 2/3 cups (14 ounces)
      canned tomatoes
2 cans (4 ounces each)
      OLD EL PASO Chopped
      Green Chilies
3/4 teaspoon salt,
      divided usage
6 eggs
1/8 teaspoon freshly ground
      black pepper
1 cup (4 ounces) shredded
      Cheddar cheese
1/4 cup butter, melted**

Preheat oven to 350°F. Fry tortillas in one inch of hot oil until crisp. Line jelly-roll pan with tortillas. Cook onions and garlic in 2 tablespoons oil until tender. Stir in tomatoes, green chilies, and 1/2 teaspoon salt. Pour over tortillas. Carefully break 1 egg on top of each tortilla. Sprinkle with remaining 1/4 teaspoon salt, pepper, and cheese. Dribble butter over cheese. Cover and bake 15 minutes. Serve immediately.

TORTILLA HASH

4 servings

**6 OLD EL PASO Corn
   Tortillas
   Vegetable oil
6 eggs, slightly beaten
1 teaspoon salt
1 can (10 ounces)
      OLD EL PASO Mild
      Enchilada Sauce
1 1/2 cups (6 ounces)
      shredded Monterey
      Jack or Mozzarella
      cheese, divided usage
1/2 cup water
1/4 cup sliced green
      onions, divided usage**

Tear tortillas into 1 1/2-inch pieces. Fry tortilla pieces in one inch of hot oil until crisp and golden. Remove with slotted spoon. Reserve 2 tablespoons oil in skillet; return tortilla pieces to skillet. Stir in eggs and salt. Cook and stir until tortilla pieces are coated and eggs are set. Stir in enchilada sauce, 1 cup cheese, water, and half the green onions. Simmer, uncovered, 15 minutes. Spoon into serving dish. Top with remaining 1/2 cup cheese and green onions.

NOTE: *To eliminate frying, 10 NACHIPS Tortilla Chips may be substituted for the 6 fried corn tortillas. Chips must be broken into pieces.*

CHILI OMELET

1 omelet

2 eggs
¼ cup (1 ounce) shredded
    Cheddar cheese
2 tablespoons sliced ripe
    olives
2 tablespoons OLD EL PASO
    Chopped Green Chilies,
    drained
⅛ teaspoon salt
    Dash black pepper
1 tablespoon butter or
    margarine
1 tablespoon PET Sour Cream
    OLD EL PASO Taco Sauce
      or OLD EL PASO Picante
    Salsa (optional)

Beat together eggs, cheese, olives, green chilies, salt, and pepper with fork until blended. In 8-inch skillet or omelet pan, heat butter just until hot enough to sizzle a drop of water. Add egg mixture; cook over medium heat. As egg mixture sets, lift edges slightly with spatula to allow uncooked portion to flow underneath. When eggs are set, remove from heat. Spoon sour cream across center. Overlap omelet and invert onto serving plate. Top omelet with taco sauce or picante salsa if desired.

Chili Omelet and Mexican Corn Muffins (page 134)

"Can she bake a cherry pie, Billy boy, Billy boy?" So runs the old song; and the pioneer housewife could. If her family was to have pie, she had no other choice. Today, the busy homemaker has several timesaving alternatives to baking pie from scratch. She can buy a frozen pie to bake fresh at home, or she can add her own filling to a store-bought frozen pie shell.

Pet has had a lot to do with creating these alternatives. And it all started in the early 1920s at a small roadside stand near Beulah, Michigan.

Mrs. Lewis Kraker certainly could bake a cherry pie. She and her husband ran the Cherry Hut stand, and tourists quickly learned that at the Cherry Hut they could buy cherry pies worth writing home about.

The Krakers' daughter, Althea, married George Petritz, and the newlyweds took over the family pie business. They had high hopes of catching the wave of what they saw as the future of the food business — frozen foods. With two employees, the bustling little business could only put out about two dozen pies a day. Cherry, apple, peach, and blueberry, the pies were filled with the bountiful produce of Michigan's fruit-growing region and were made from the Kraker family recipe. Each day George drove to Detroit to sell their delicious fruit pies. The popularity of their pies grew, and the business did so well that they soon were able to acquire a major producer of sour red cherries and apple juice — Crystal Canning Company.

In those days, Pet was called Pet Milk Company and our only products were evaporated milk and milk-related items. But we were on the verge of a whole new era of growth and diversification. Our first big step into that exciting period came in 1955, with the purchase of the business of George and Althea Petritz. We had noticed the fine little company and its top-notch pies, and its name was a natural for us: "PET" to identify the company, and the "-RITZ" with its promise of an especially elegant pie.

We moved Pet-Ritz to a plant near Frankfort, Michigan in the heart of the Midwest's fruit country. Over the years we've expanded our frozen-food operations in Frankfort and added other plants in Pennsylvania, Georgia and Oklahoma. To the original line of luscious fruit pies, we've added mince and pumpkin pies, fruit cobblers, and our most popular item, PET-RITZ frozen pie crust shells, in both regular and deep-dish varieties.

More recently, some exciting new winners have joined the Pet-Ritz lineup: cream pies in graham cracker crusts, fancy crust pies with lattice tops, a whole-wheat pie crust with a delicious nutty flavor, and a special pie shell made with all-vegetable shortening. Today, Pet-Ritz is America's largest manufacturer of pie crust shells, selling more pie shells than any other company.

Maybe one reason for the tremendous success of our pie crusts is that so many homemakers agree that the creative part of making a pie goes into the filling. Pies made with a PET-RITZ shell are essentially home-made, and to a guest or family member eating a wedge of delicious, fresh-baked pie, the question, "Does she or doesn't she make her own crust?" matters not a bit.

"You could fool Grandma," declared a 1970s ad for DOWNYFLAKE Waffles. You could fool her, that is, if she didn't catch you slipping the frozen waffles into the toaster — because DOWNYFLAKE Waffles taste as though they've been made from scratch. And Grandma, we've found, is like everyone else, happy to save time and eliminate another bulky tool and another kitchen chore.

Downyflake Foods, Inc., joined the Pet family in 1963. Our customers trusted the Downyflake name, and when Downyflake and Pet came together, we were able to provide a fine line of high-quality breakfast foods. Since then we've never stopped thinking up products to help make breakfast quick and easy. Some favorites have been French toast, pan-cakes, breads, and always our waffles — waffles made with buttermilk, waffles fla-vored with blueberries, round waffles and square waffles. Packaged in bags rather than boxes, our waffles appeal to the pennywise homemaker — an economy-size package is easily collapsed, resealed, and popped in the freezer for tomorrow's breakfast. Consumer support through the

The day you find colonial tenderness in a new, bigger frozen waffle... it's Downyflake!

years has made DOWNYFLAKE a leading waffle in American homes. Breakfast, of course, is DOWNYFLAKE'S "main event," but waffles have begun to appear in delightful new company as well — as the star attrac-tion in mouthwatering desserts and a whole array of other tempting recipes.

Dessert may still be a leisurely affair, but more and more Americans are eating breakfast "on the run" — and with DOWNYFLAKE frozen breakfast items making that most important meal of the day simple to prepare, and simply delicious, we're sure even Grandma would approve.

WAFFLES SUPREME

4 open-faced sandwiches

4 slices Canadian bacon
4 DOWNYFLAKE Waffles,
    any variety
4 slices Cheddar cheese
¼ cup OLD EL PASO Taco
    Sauce or OLD EL PASO
    Picante Salsa

Cook Canadian bacon until heated through. Heat waffles according to package directions. Top waffles with Canadian bacon, Cheddar cheese, and taco sauce or picante salsa. Serve immediately.

PEANUT-HONEY TRIANGLES

4 servings

½ cup creamy peanut butter
3 tablespoons honey
3 tablespoons chopped
    peanuts
4 DOWNYFLAKE Waffles,
    toasted

Blend peanut butter and honey. Stir in peanuts. Spread evenly on waffles. Cut waffles diagonally in triangles. Place in broiler 2 to 4 minutes or until lightly browned.

NOTE: *Crunchy peanut butter can be substituted for creamy; omit nuts.*

WAFFLE OLE

4 sandwiches

4 eggs
¼ cup PET Evaporated Milk
8 DOWNYFLAKE Homemade
    Style Waffles
4 slices Monterey Jack cheese
    OLD EL PASO Taco Sauce
    or OLD EL PASO Picante
    Salsa

Beat together eggs and evaporated milk. Scramble over low heat until firm. Heat waffles according to package directions. Spread scrambled eggs on 4 waffles. Top each with 1 cheese slice, taco sauce or picante salsa, and 1 waffle. Serve immediately.

HEARTY MAN SANDWICH
4 sandwiches

4 sausage patties
8 ROMAN MEAL Waffles
¼ cup maple syrup
4 slices process American
   cheese

Cook sausage patties until brown. Drain. Heat waffles according to package directions. Top each waffle with 1 sausage patty, syrup, 1 cheese slice, and 1 waffle. Serve immediately.

FIESTA SANDWICH
4 sandwiches

4 eggs
¼ cup PET Evaporated Milk
¼ cup OLD EL PASO
   Chopped Green Chilies
4 slices ham
8 DOWNYFLAKE Waffles,
   any variety
¼ cup OLD EL PASO Picante
   Salsa or OLD EL PASO
   Taco Sauce

Beat together eggs, evaporated milk, and green chilies. Scramble over low heat until firm. Grill ham until heated through. Heat waffles according to package directions. Spread scrambled eggs on 4 waffles. Top each with 1 ham slice, picante salsa or taco sauce, and 1 waffle. Serve immediately.

BREAKFAST REUBEN
4 breakfast sandwiches

4 hot dogs
4 DOWNYFLAKE Homemade
   Style Waffles
½ cup drained sauerkraut
4 slices Swiss cheese

Cook hot dogs until heated through. Heat waffles according to package directions. Slit hot dogs in half lengthwise and place 1 on each waffle. Spoon 2 tablespoons sauerkraut over each hot dog and top with 1 slice cheese. Serve open-faced.

INTERNATIONAL COMBO

4 open-faced sandwiches

4 eggs
1/4 cup PET Evaporated Milk
8 slices bacon
4 slices DOWNYFLAKE
   French Toast
4 slices process American
   cheese
4 slices tomato (optional)

Beat together eggs and evaporated milk. Scramble over low heat until firm. Fry bacon until crisp. Drain. Heat French toast according to package directions. Spread scrambled eggs evenly onto 4 slices French toast. Top each with 2 slices bacon, 1 slice American cheese, and 1 slice tomato if desired.

PANCAKES

Eighteen 4-inch pancakes

(photograph on page 57)

2 cups baking mix
1 small can (5.33 fluid
   ounces) PET Evaporated
   Milk
2/3 cup water
1 egg

Mix all ingredients until moistened. On hot, slightly greased griddle or heavy skillet, fry pancakes until bubbles appear and edges are set. Turn and brown other side. Serve hot.

NOTE: *Overmixing the batter will toughen the pancakes.*

HEARTY WAFFLES

6 large waffles, 4 sections each

2 cups all-purpose flour
2 tablespoons sugar
4 teaspoons baking powder
1 teaspoon salt
3 eggs, separated
1 cup PET Evaporated Milk
1 cup water
1/2 cup shortening, melted

In large bowl, stir together flour, sugar, baking powder, and salt. In another bowl, beat egg yolks. Add evaporated milk, water, and shortening; beat until smooth. Pour liquid mixture into flour mixture and mix. Beat egg whites until stiff peaks form. Fold egg whites into batter. Bake in hot waffle iron until golden brown.

FRENCH TOAST

4 servings, 2 slices each

1 egg, well beaten
3/4 cup PET Evaporated Milk
1/4 teaspoon salt
8 slices bread
 Butter or margarine

In shallow dish, beat together egg, evaporated milk, and salt. Dip bread slices in mixture, 1 at a time, moistening both sides. Melt enough butter to cover bottom of large skillet. In skillet, brown bread slices on both sides. Add more butter as needed. Serve French toast warm.

ALOHA TREAT

4 open-faced sandwiches   *(photograph on page 57)*

4 slices ham
4 ROMAN MEAL Waffles
1 package (3 ounces)
 cream cheese, softened
1/2 cup drained crushed
 pineapple

Grill ham until heated through. Heat waffles according to package directions. Spread each waffle evenly with cream cheese. Layer with grilled ham and crushed pineapple. Serve immediately.

APPLE NUT COFFEE CAKE

9 servings

1 cup all-purpose flour
1/2 cup granulated sugar
2 teaspoons baking powder
2 medium apples, peeled,
 cored, and chopped
1/2 cup chopped pecans
1/2 cup PET Evaporated Milk
1 teaspoon vanilla

Topping:

1/3 cup all-purpose flour
2 tablespoons brown sugar
2 tablespoons butter or
 margarine

Preheat oven to 400°F. In large bowl, stir together flour, granulated sugar, and baking powder. In separate bowl, mix apples, pecans, evaporated milk, and vanilla. Stir into flour mixture until well mixed. Pour into greased 9-inch square baking pan. For topping, combine flour, brown sugar, and butter until crumbly. Sprinkle over batter. Bake 30 to 35 minutes or until toothpick inserted in center comes out clean.

TRADITIONAL CINNAMON COFFEE CAKE
9 servings

2 cups all-purpose flour
1/2 cup sugar, divided usage
4 teaspoons baking powder
1/2 teaspoon salt
1 egg, well beaten
1 1/4 cups PET Evaporated Milk
1/4 cup water
2 tablespoons shortening, melted
2 teaspoons ground cinnamon

Preheat oven to 425°F. In large bowl, stir together flour, ¼ cup sugar, baking powder, and salt. In separate bowl, mix egg, evaporated milk, water, and shortening. Add liquid mixture to flour mixture and mix just until moistened. Pour batter into greased 8-inch square baking pan. Combine remaining ¼ cup sugar and cinnamon and sprinkle on top of cake. Using a knife, swirl cinnamon-sugar into batter. Bake 25 minutes or until top springs back when lightly touched.

GLAZED NUT COFFEE CAKE
9 servings

2/3 cup dark corn syrup
2/3 cup firmly packed brown sugar
2/3 cup chopped pecans
2 tablespoons butter or margarine, melted
3 cups biscuit mix
1/3 cup granulated sugar
1 cup PET Evaporated Milk
2 tablespoons water

Preheat oven to 400°F. In small bowl, mix corn syrup, brown sugar, pecans, and butter. Spread mixture evenly over bottom of greased 9-inch square baking pan. In large bowl, combine biscuit mix and granulated sugar. Stir in evaporated milk and water; combine only until ingredients are moistened. Spread batter over nut mixture. Bake 35 to 40 minutes or until toothpick inserted near center comes out clean. Let cake cool 5 minutes and then invert onto serving plate. Serve cake warm.

Dutch Treat
In colonial days, a special wedding gift for a Dutch bride in New York was a waffle iron carved with her initials and wedding date. To the Dutch goes the credit for introducing waffles to America.

HIDDEN JAM MUFFINS
12 muffins

2 cups all-purpose flour
¹/₂ cup sugar, divided usage
4 teaspoons baking powder
1 teaspoon salt
1 small can (5.33 fluid ounces) PET Evaporated Milk
¹/₃ cup water
¹/₄ cup shortening, melted
1 egg
¹/₄ cup jam, any flavor
¹/₂ teaspoon ground cinnamon

Preheat oven to 400°F. In medium bowl, combine flour, ¼ cup sugar, baking powder, and salt. In separate bowl, combine evaporated milk, water, shortening, and egg. Add liquid mixture to flour mixture and mix just until moistened. Spoon batter into greased muffin tins, filling one-third full. Drop about 1 teaspoon jam into center of each muffin. Spoon remaining batter over jam, filling each tin two-thirds full. Combine remaining ¼ cup sugar and cinnamon; sprinkle over muffins. Bake 20 to 25 minutes or until brown.

SOUR CREAM BRAN MUFFINS
12 muffins

1 ¹/₄ cups sifted all-purpose flour
¹/₃ cup sugar
1 tablespoon baking powder
¹/₂ teaspoon baking soda
¹/₂ teaspoon ground cinnamon
¹/₂ teaspoon salt
1 egg
1 container (16 ounces) PET Sour Cream
¹/₄ cup vegetable oil
2 cups bran flakes

Preheat oven to 400°F. In large bowl, sift together flour, sugar, baking powder, baking soda, cinnamon, and salt. In small bowl, beat egg. Gradually stir in sour cream and oil. Add to dry ingredients and mix just until moistened. Add bran flakes. Spoon batter into greased muffin tins. Bake 20 to 25 minutes or until toothpick inserted in muffins comes out clean. Serve warm.

Blueberry Muffins (page 76), Sour Cream Bran Muffins, Hidden Jam Muffins

BLUEBERRY MUFFINS

12 muffins   *(photograph on page 74)*

1³/₄ cups all-purpose flour
¹/₄ cup sugar
1 tablespoon baking powder
1 teaspoon salt
1 egg, beaten
¹/₂ cup PET Evaporated Milk
¹/₂ cup water
2 tablespoons butter or
      margarine, melted
1 cup blueberries

Preheat oven to 400°F. In large bowl, combine flour, sugar, baking powder, and salt. In small bowl, combine egg, evaporated milk, water, and butter. Add milk mixture to flour mixture and stir just until moistened. Gently mix in blueberries. Spoon batter into greased muffin tins, filling ⅔ full. Bake 20 to 25 minutes or until lightly browned.

SOUR CREAM BISCUITS

10 biscuits   *(photograph on page 57)*

2 to 2¹/₂ cups biscuit mix
1 can (8 ounces) PET
      Imitation Sour Cream

Preheat oven to 450°F. Combine biscuit mix and sour cream, adding enough biscuit mix to form a soft dough. Turn dough out onto floured board. Knead 10 times. Roll out to ½-inch thickness. Cut biscuits with floured biscuit cutter. Carefully place biscuits on ungreased cookie sheet. Bake 8 to 10 minutes or until golden brown.

PARSLEY BISCUITS

10 to 12 biscuits

2 cups biscuit mix
1 tablespoon diced parsley
1 small can (5.33 fluid
      ounces) PET Evaporated
      Milk

Preheat oven to 450°F. In mixing bowl, combine biscuit mix and parsley. Stir in evaporated milk. Turn dough out onto lightly floured board. Knead a few seconds or until dough is smooth. Roll to ½-inch thickness. With floured 2-inch cutter, cut into rounds. Place rounds on ungreased cookie sheet. Bake 8 to 10 minutes or until brown.

Buttery Almond Pound Cake (page 87), with Hot Fudge Sauce (page 152), Hearty Vegetable Soup (page 78), Chocolate Mocha Drink (page 84)

To Warm the Wonders
of Winter

HEARTY VEGETABLE SOUP

6 servings   *(photograph on page 77)*

6 slices bacon
1 can (1 pound) tomatoes, cut into pieces
1 can (1 pound) whole-kernel corn
1 can (1 pound) sliced carrots, drained
1 can (1 pound) green beans
1 can (10¾ ounces) condensed cream of potato soup
1 cup (4 ounces) shredded process American cheese
1 cup PET Evaporated Milk
1 tablespoon sugar
1 tablespoon minced onion
½ teaspoon salt
½ teaspoon paprika
2 drops hot pepper sauce

Cook bacon until crisp. Drain, and crumble. In 3-quart saucepan, mix all ingredients except bacon. Heat mixture over medium heat until steaming, but do not boil. To serve, garnish with crumbled bacon.

CREAMY CHICKEN POTATO SOUP

Six 1-cup servings

4 cups diced potatoes
1 medium onion, chopped
¼ cup vegetable oil
1½ cups chopped cooked chicken
1½ cups chicken broth
2 teaspoons parsley flakes
2 teaspoons salt
1 tall can (12 fluid ounces) PET Evaporated Milk

In large saucepan, cook potatoes and onion in hot oil just until potatoes begin to brown. Add chicken, chicken broth, parsley, and salt. Bring mixture to a boil. Lower heat, cover, and simmer about 20 minutes or until potatoes are tender. Stir in evaporated milk. Heat soup until steaming, but do not boil.

SAVORY FISH CHOWDER
6 servings

4 cups water
2 teaspoons AC'CENT
   Flavor Enhancer
3 pounds cod or haddock
   fillets, cut in 2-inch
   pieces
⅛ pound fat salt pork,
   diced
3 large onions, thinly
   sliced
3 cups potatoes, peeled
   and diced
1 tall can (12 fluid ounces)
   PET Evaporated Milk
1 can (8 ounces) tomato
   sauce
¼ teaspoon white pepper

In large saucepan, combine water and AC'CENT; bring to a boil. Add fish; reduce heat and simmer 10 minutes. Drain fish and reserve liquid. In deep kettle over medium heat, fry salt pork until golden. Add onions, cooking until tender. Add potatoes and reserved fish liquid; bring mixture to a boil. Reduce heat, cover, and simmer about 20 minutes or until potatoes are tender. Add fish, evaporated milk, tomato sauce, and pepper. Simmer 5 minutes; do not boil.

BROCCOLI MUSHROOM SOUP
4 servings

1 can (10¾ ounces)
   chicken broth
1 package (10 ounces)
   frozen chopped broccoli,
   unthawed
1 tablespoon minced onion
1 can (10¾ ounces) cream of
   mushroom soup
1 cup PET Evaporated Milk
Salt and freshly ground
   black pepper to taste
Fresh parsley sprigs

In 3-quart saucepan, combine chicken broth, broccoli, and onion. Cover and simmer 15 minutes. Break apart broccoli, and simmer an additional 10 minutes or until tender. Stir in mushroom soup, evaporated milk, salt, and pepper. Heat mixture until steaming, but do not boil. To serve, garnish each bowl with a parsley sprig.

Gift from the Sea
Long ago, French fishermen would throw part of their catch into *la chaudière*, a huge copper pot, so that the whole town could share in celebrating the fishing fleet's safe return. The custom and the name of the copper pot traveled to Canada and then down the coast to New England, where *chaudiere*, a concoction of fish and shellfish, became known as chowder.

VEGETABLE MEAT STEW

6 servings

1 pound beef for stew
2 tablespoons all-purpose flour
1 1/2 teaspoons salt
1 teaspoon AC'CENT Flavor Enhancer
1/8 teaspoon freshly ground black pepper
3 tablespoons vegetable oil
1/4 cup chopped onion
3 cups water
1 garlic clove, minced
1 bay leaf
1 teaspoon thyme
4 small potatoes, peeled and cubed
4 carrots, peeled and chopped or 12 mini-carrots, peeled
1 cup frozen peas, defrosted
1/2 cup PET Evaporated Milk

Cut meat into cubes. Roll into mixture of flour, salt, AC'CENT, and pepper. Reserve flour mixture. Brown meat slowly in hot oil. Sprinkle any remaining flour mixture over meat. Toss to coat meat. Add onion; cook until limp. Add water, garlic, bay leaf, and thyme. Bring to a boil. Cover and cook over low heat 1 hour. Add potatoes, carrots, and additional water as needed. Cover and cook 15 minutes. Add peas and continue to cook about 10 minutes or until vegetables are tender. Stir in evaporated milk. Heat until steaming hot, but do not boil. Remove bay leaf. Serve hot.

COUNTRY FARE

4 servings

6 slices bacon, diced
1 can (17 ounces) cream-style corn
1 tall can (12 fluid ounces) PET Evaporated Milk
1 can (10 3/4 ounces) condensed cream of potato soup
1 cup water
1 1/2 teaspoons salt
   Dash freshly ground black pepper

In 3-quart saucepan, brown bacon. Stir in corn, evaporated milk, potato soup, water, salt, and pepper. Heat, stirring often, until hot, but do not boil.

MICROWAVE DIRECTIONS: *In deep 3-quart microwave safe casserole, microwave bacon on HIGH 3 minutes or until limp. Stir in corn, evaporated milk, potato soup, water, salt, and pepper. Mix well. Microwave on HIGH 10 minutes. Stir 1 to 2 times during cooking time. Let stand 5 minutes before serving.*

Vegetable Meat Stew, Sour Cream Biscuits (page 76)

82

CRAB BISQUE

6 servings

¹/₂ cup butter or margarine
¹/₄ cup chopped onion
2 tablespoons all-purpose
**   flour**
¹/₂ teaspoon curry powder
3 cups whole milk
1 teaspoon salt
¹/₈ teaspoon ground
**   coriander**
¹/₈ teaspoon white pepper
2 cans (6 ounces each)
**   ORLEANS White or Lump**
**   Crab Meat, drained**
1 tall can (12 fluid ounces)
**   PET Evaporated Milk**
2 tablespoons sherry
**   (optional)**

In 3-quart saucepan, melt butter. Sauté onion in melted butter until tender. Add flour and curry powder; cook 5 minutes. Add whole milk, salt, coriander, and pepper. Bring mixture to a boil. Lower heat and stir in crab meat, evaporated milk, and sherry if desired. Continue to heat until soup is steaming, but do not boil. Serve immediately.

POTAGE ST. GERMAIN

4 servings

1 tall can (12 fluid ounces)
**   PET Evaporated Milk**
1 can (11¹/₂ ounces) split pea
**   soup with ham and bacon**
1 can (10¹/₂ ounces) cream of
**   chicken soup**
¹/₂ cup water
¹/₂ cup cooked chopped
**   carrots**

In 3-quart saucepan, combine all ingredients. Stirring occasionally, heat soup until steaming, but do not boil. Serve hot.

MICROWAVE DIRECTIONS: *In deep 2-quart microwave safe casserole, combine all ingredients. Microwave on HIGH 10 minutes or until heated through. Stir 1 to 2 times during cooking time. Let stand 5 minutes before serving.*

Crab Bisque

84

CHOCOLATE MOCHA DRINK

4 servings   *(photograph on page 77)*

¹/₃ cup water
¹/₄ cup sugar
2 tablespoons unsweetened
   cocoa powder
¹/₂ cup PET Evaporated Milk
2 tablespoons WHITMAN'S
   Semi-Sweet Chocolate
   Chips
   Hot coffee
   PET WHIP Non-Dairy
   Whipped Topping,
   thawed

In saucepan, combine water, sugar, and cocoa. Simmer mixture over medium heat 2 minutes, stirring frequently. Reduce heat and add evaporated milk in a slow stream, beating vigorously, until well combined. Add 2 tablespoons chocolate chips. Continue to heat until chocolate is completely melted, but do not boil. Divide mixture among 4 heatproof glasses and then fill with hot coffee. Garnish each drink with a dollop of whipped topping, and sprinkle with chocolate chips.

RICH AND CREAMY COCOA

4 servings

2 cups hot water
¹/₄ cup unsweetened cocoa
   powder
¹/₄ cup sugar
¹/₄ teaspoon salt
¹/₄ teaspoon ground
   cinnamon
¹/₈ teaspoon ground nutmeg
2 cups PET Evaporated Milk
6 large marshmallows
³/₄ teaspoon vanilla

In heavy saucepan, mix hot water, cocoa, sugar, salt, cinnamon, and nutmeg. Over medium heat, cook mixture to a boil. Boil 5 minutes, stirring frequently. Reduce heat and add evaporated milk and marshmallows. Heat slowly until marshmallows are dissolved. Add vanilla. Remove from heat and beat one minute with rotary beater. Serve at once.

Depression Drink

PET Evaporated Milk replaced fresh milk for millions of Americans during the Great Depression of the 1930s. Low in cost, high in nutrition, portable, and long-lasting, PET Milk met all the tests of that economic era. When overloaded jalopies headed west bearing families in search of a better life, nearly every one carried a supply of evaporated milk.

OLD-FASHIONED BREAD PUDDING
8 servings

¹/₄ cup butter or margarine, softened
8 slices bread, toasted
¹/₃ cup raisins (optional)
4 eggs
¹/₂ cup sugar
¹/₄ teaspoon salt
2 cups PET Evaporated Milk
2 cups water
2 teaspoons vanilla
4 teaspoons sugar
¹/₄ teaspoon ground cinnamon

Butter toasted bread. Cut bread into cubes, and place in greased 13 × 9-inch baking dish. Sprinkle raisins over toast, if desired. Thoroughly beat eggs, ½ cup sugar, salt, evaporated milk, water, and vanilla. Pour mixture over toast and let stand 10 minutes. Combine remaining 4 teaspoons sugar and cinnamon; sprinkle over bread. Place dish in shallow baking pan. Pour hot water into pan to a depth of one inch. Bake at 325°F 1 hour to 1 hour 5 minutes or until knife inserted one inch from edge comes out clean. Remove dish from water. Serve pudding warm or chilled.

Fig. 1: Inserting knife

Fig. 2: Clean knife

CAFE ROYALE

5 servings

4 cups water
1/2 cup (3 ounces) WHITMAN'S Semi-Sweet Chocolate Chips
1/2 cup sugar
1/2 teaspoon ground cinnamon
1/4 teaspoon ground nutmeg
1 tablespoon instant coffee granules
1 cup PET Evaporated Milk
1/2 teaspoon vanilla
1/4 cup Kahlua or other coffee-flavored liqueur (optional)
PET WHIP Non-Dairy Whipped Topping, thawed
Ground cinnamon

In heavy saucepan, combine water, chocolate chips, sugar, cinnamon, and nutmeg. Bring mixture to a boil over medium heat, stirring frequently. Continue to boil until chocolate is completely melted. Add coffee granules, stirring until dissolved. Reduce heat and gradually stir in evaporated milk. Stir in vanilla and liqueur if desired. Pour into mugs and top with whipped topping and sprinkle with cinnamon.

BUTTERY ALMOND POUND CAKE

12 servings   *(photograph on page 77)*

1/2 cup sliced almonds
3 1/2 cups all-purpose flour
2 teaspoons baking powder
3/4 cup butter or margarine
2 cups sugar
2 eggs
1 small can (5.33 fluid ounces) PET Evaporated Milk
1/2 cup water
1 teaspoon vanilla
Hot Fudge Sauce (optional, pg. 152)

Generously grease 10-inch tube pan. Sprinkle sliced almonds into greased pan, shaking to cover bottom and sides. Preheat oven to 350°F. Combine flour and baking powder; set aside. In large mixing bowl, cream butter. Gradually add sugar and beat until fluffy. Beat in eggs. Mix in half the flour mixture. Stir in evaporated milk, water, and vanilla. Mix in remaining flour and blend well. Pour batter into almond-lined pan. Bake 40 to 45 minutes or until toothpick inserted near center comes out clean. Top individual cake slices with Hot Fudge Sauce if desired.

Café Royale Sugar Cookies (page 17)

88

PUMPKIN RAISIN COOKIES
4 dozen cookies

**2 1/2 cups firmly packed
  brown sugar
2 cups biscuit mix
1 teaspoon pumpkin pie
  spice
1 can (16 ounces) solid-pack
  pumpkin
1 small can (5.33 fluid
  ounces) PET Evaporated
  Milk
1/2 cup vegetable oil
3 cups rolled oats
1 cup raisins**

Preheat oven to 375°F. Stir together brown sugar, biscuit mix, and pumpkin pie spice. Stir in pumpkin, evaporated milk, and oil. Stir until smooth. Mix in oats and raisins; mix until well blended. Drop by rounded teaspoonfuls onto greased cookie sheets. Bake 10 minutes or until lightly browned. Cool, and frost each cookie with 1 tablespoon Creamy Orange Frosting.

CREAMY ORANGE FROSTING
2 cups

**1/2 cup butter or margarine,
  softened
1/4 cup PET Evaporated Milk
1 teaspoon orange extract
4 cups (1 pound)
  confectioners sugar,
  sifted**

In small mixing bowl, combine butter, evaporated milk, and orange extract. Gradually add confectioners sugar, beating until smooth after each addition.

PEACHES AND CREAM
Four 1/2-cup servings or 2 cups sauce

**1/4 cup sugar
1 tablespoon cornstarch
1/2 teaspoon ground
  cinnamon
1/4 teaspoon ground nutmeg
1 can (16 ounces) sliced
  peaches, drained,
    1/4 cup juice reserved
1/2 cup PET Whipping Cream
1 tablespoon brandy
  (optional)**

In medium saucepan, combine sugar, cornstarch, cinnamon, and nutmeg. Stir in cream, and reserved juice. Bring to a boil over medium heat. Boil 1 minute. Stir in peach slices. Heat until peaches are warm. Stir in brandy if desired. Serve immediately.

NOTE: *This recipe makes a dish delicious by itself, or as a sauce over brown bread or ice cream.*

PUMPKIN CUSTARD
8 servings

1 **can (16 ounces) solid-pack pumpkin**
1 **egg, beaten**
3 **tablespoons all-purpose flour**
1 **teaspoon salt**
1 **teaspoon ground cinnamon**
1/2 **teaspoon allspice**
1/2 **teaspoon ground cloves**
1/4 **teaspoon ground ginger**
1 **tall can (12 fluid ounces) PET Evaporated Milk**
1 **cup sugar PET WHIP Non-Dairy Whipped Topping, thawed**

Preheat oven to 350°F. Beat together pumpkin and egg. Mix in flour, salt, cinnamon, allspice, cloves, and ginger. Stir in evaporated milk and sugar. Beat mixture until sugar is dissolved. Pour into 8 custard cups. Place cups in large baking dish. Pour one inch hot water around cups. Bake 1 hour or until knife inserted one inch from edge comes out clean. Serve topped with PET WHIP.

BOSTON BROWN BREAD DESSERT
4 small loaves

2 **cups whole bran cereal**
2 **cups PET Buttermilk**
2 1/2 **cups all-purpose flour**
1 **cup chopped pecans**
1 **cup raisins (optional)**
1 **cup firmly packed brown sugar**
2 **teaspoons baking soda**
1/4 **teaspoon salt**
2 **eggs, slightly beaten Spice and Raisin Sauce (page 152)**

Preheat oven to 350°F. In large bowl, combine cereal and buttermilk. Allow cereal to stand about 5 minutes or until moisture is absorbed. Stir together flour, pecans, raisins if desired, brown sugar, baking soda, and salt. Add flour mixture and eggs to cereal mixture and mix just until moistened. Divide batter among 4 greased 1-pound vegetable or fruit cans. Bake on cookie sheet 50 to 55 minutes or until toothpick inserted near center comes out clean. Remove bread from cans and allow to cool. Slice bread and serve topped with Spice and Raisin Sauce.

FRESH APPLE CRISP

8 servings

3 pounds apples, peeled, cored, and sliced
¹/₂ cup butter or margarine
¹/₂ cup all-purpose flour
¹/₂ cup firmly packed brown sugar
1 teaspoon ground cinnamon
¹/₂ teaspoon ground nutmeg
2 cups HEARTLAND Natural Cereal, Plain or Coconut
PET Vanilla Ice Cream

Preheat oven to 375°F. Generously butter an 11 × 7-inch baking dish. Arrange apple slices in dish. In bowl, combine butter, flour, brown sugar, cinnamon, and nutmeg until crumbly. Stir in HEARTLAND cereal. Sprinkle over apples, making sure edges are covered. Bake 25 to 30 minutes or until crumb top is browned. Serve warm with ice cream.

NUTTY APPLESAUCE CAKE

12 servings

2 cups all-purpose flour
1 teaspoon ground cinnamon
¹/₂ teaspoon ground cloves
¹/₂ teaspoon salt
1 ¹/₄ cups applesauce
1 ¹/₂ teaspoons baking soda
¹/₂ cup butter or margarine
1 cup sugar
¹/₂ cup PET Evaporated Milk
¹/₂ cup broken pecans
¹/₂ cup raisins (optional)
PET WHIP Non-Dairy Whipped Topping, thawed (optional)

Preheat oven to 350°F. In small bowl, combine flour, cinnamon, cloves, and salt. In separate bowl, combine applesauce and baking soda. In large mixing bowl, cream butter. Gradually add sugar, beating until fluffy. Add half the flour mixture. Beat in evaporated milk and applesauce mixture. Mix in remaining flour mixture and blend well. Stir in pecans and raisins if desired. Pour into 13 × 9-inch baking pan. Bake 30 to 35 minutes or until toothpick inserted near center comes out clean. Serve cake plain or topped with PET WHIP, if desired.

Fresh Apple Crisp with PET Vanilla Ice Cream

GINGERBREAD
9 servings

1 1/2 cups all-purpose flour
1/2 cup granulated sugar
1 teaspoon baking soda
*1 teaspoon ground
    cinnamon*
1/2 teaspoon ground ginger
1/4 teaspoon salt
1/2 cup light molasses
1/4 cup butter or margarine
*1/4 cup firmly packed brown
    sugar*
*1 small can (5.33 fluid
    ounces) PET Evaporated
    Milk*
1 egg, well beaten
*PET WHIP Non-Dairy
    Whipped Topping,
    thawed (optional)*

Preheat oven to 350°F. In large bowl, stir together flour, granulated sugar, baking soda, cinnamon, ginger, and salt. In small saucepan, melt molasses, butter, and brown sugar. Add evaporated milk to warm mixture, then beat in egg. Pour molasses mixture over dry ingredients. Beat with electric mixer on LOW until moistened. Beat on HIGH 2 additional minutes. Pour batter into greased 8-inch square baking pan. Bake 30 to 35 minutes or until toothpick inserted near center comes out clean. Top with PET WHIP or glaze warm cake with Creamy Vanilla Glaze.

CREAMY VANILLA GLAZE

*1 1/2 cups sifted confectioners
    sugar*
*2 tablespoons PET
    Evaporated Milk*
*1 teaspoon vanilla
    Dash salt*

Combine all ingredients. Beat until smooth. Glaze warm cake.

CAFE AU LAIT

Hot strong coffee
PET Evaporated Milk

Mix equal amounts of coffee and evaporated milk in coffee cup. Serve with sugar.

*Garden Shrimp Salad (page 95), Creamy Pistachio Pie (page 108),
Orange Frost (page 105), Deviled Ham Bunwiches (page 103)*

To Beat the Heat
of Summer

ASPARAGUS SALAD

4 to 6 servings

**1 pound fresh asparagus,
    cut diagonally into
    1-inch lengths
2 medium carrots, cut
    in matchsticks
4 cups boiling water
4 cups ice water
1 teaspoon sesame seeds
1/2 teaspoon AC'CENT
    Flavor Enhancer
2 teaspoons lemon juice
1 teaspoon sesame seed oil
1/2 teaspoon soy sauce
    Shredded cabbage**

Plunge asparagus and carrots into boiling water. Boil 1 minute. Drain, and immediately plunge vegetables into ice water to cool. In small mixing bowl, combine sesame seeds, AC'CENT, lemon juice, sesame seed oil, and soy sauce; mix well. Drain vegetables again and place in large bowl. Pour dressing mixture over vegetables; toss lightly. Serve on shredded cabbage.

In Louisiana lakes and the deeper Gulf waters, shrimp are harvested by trawler in the spring and the fall. They are washed, cooked, inspected, sorted, sealed in cans, and sterilized — often in less than an hour from the time the shrimp are unloaded at our processing plants. This "fresh-catch" quality has made Pet's ORLEANS shrimp the most popular brand in America.

Over forty years ago, two young men set up a shrimp operation in Louisiana, and by 1971, when ORLEANS joined the Pet family, their fine canned seafood products were enjoying widespread popularity. Since then, with Pet's support, the popularity of the ORLEANS brand has sky-rocketed as consumers have discovered that shrimp are low in calories, high in nutrition, and the perfect food in a variety of salads, party hors d'oeuvres, and light meals at home.

Today, shrimp isn't our only specialty canned seafood product — OR-LEANS Louisiana Oysters, Smoked Oysters, Clams, and Crab Meat are other seasonal delicacies with year-round popularity.

GARDEN SHRIMP SALAD

Five ½-cup servings (photograph on page 93)

- 2 cans (4¼ ounces each) ORLEANS Deveined Medium Shrimp
- 2 cups shell macaroni, cooked
- 1 cup (4 ounces) shredded Cheddar cheese
- ¾ cup frozen peas, thawed
- ½ cup celery pieces (¼-inch diagonal pieces)
- ⅓ cup PET Evaporated Milk
- ⅓ cup mayonnaise or salad dressing
- ¼ cup sweet pickle relish
- 1 tablespoon chopped pimiento
- 2 teaspoons minced onion
- 2 teaspoons prepared mustard
- ¼ teaspoon salt
- 3 to 4 drops hot pepper sauce
  Few grains black pepper
  Lettuce leaves

Rinse shrimp under cold running water. Drain. In large bowl, mix all ingredients except lettuce. Cover and refrigerate 1½ to 2 hours or until salad is well chilled. Serve shrimp salad in a lettuce cup.

CHICKEN SUMMER SALAD

4 servings

- 1¼ cups PET Cottage Cheese
- 1 can (4¾ ounces) UNDERWOOD Chunky Chicken Spread
- ¼ cup chopped celery
- ¼ cup chopped water chestnuts
- 1 tablespoon chopped onion
- 1 teaspoon dried chives
- 8 slices canned pineapple rings
  Lettuce leaves

In small mixing bowl, combine cottage cheese, chicken spread, celery, water chestnuts, onion, and chives. Arrange 2 pineapple rings per serving on a bed of lettuce. Scoop chicken salad mixture on top of pineapple. Refrigerate until well chilled.

SHRIMP/SPINACH SALAD

6 servings

**1 pound spinach or
leaf lettuce
5 slices bacon
1/4 cup wine vinegar
2 tablespoons water
2 tablespoons firmly
packed brown sugar
1/2 teaspoon dry mustard
1/4 teaspoon salt
1/8 teaspoon freshly
ground pepper
1 can (4 1/4 ounces)
ORLEANS Deveined
Medium Shrimp
3 eggs, hard-cooked and
chopped
6 fresh mushrooms, sliced**

Wash spinach and remove stems, or clean lettuce. Pat dry, and break into bite-size pieces. Meanwhile, fry bacon until crisp. Drain bacon, reserving 2 tablespoons drippings. Crumble cooled bacon. In small skillet, prepare dressing by combining reserved bacon drippings, vinegar, water, brown sugar, dry mustard, salt, and pepper. Bring mixture to a boil. Remove from heat and allow to cool. Rinse shrimp under cold running water; drain thoroughly. In large bowl, toss together greens, dressing, and shrimp. Garnish with chopped eggs, crumbled bacon, and sliced mushrooms. Serve immediately.

CREAMY CUCUMBER SALAD

Six 1/2-cup servings   *(photograph on page 211)*

**1 container (8 ounces)
PET Sour Cream
1/4 cup minced green onions
1/4 cup chopped green
pepper
2 tablespoons tarragon
vinegar
1 teaspoon dillweed
1 teaspoon salt
1/8 teaspoon freshly ground
black pepper
2 medium cucumbers,
peeled and sliced**

In medium bowl, combine sour cream, green onions, green pepper, vinegar, dillweed, salt, and pepper. Add cucumber slices and blend well. Cover tightly and refrigerate 2 to 3 hours or until chilled.

Shrimp/Spinach Salad

CALICO SALAD

Eight ½-cup servings

1 can (10 ounces) lima beans,
    or 1 package (10 ounces)
    frozen baby lima beans
1 package (10 ounces)
    frozen peas, thawed
1 jar (2 ounces) sliced
    pimientos
½ cup slivered almonds
½ cup PET Sour Cream
¼ cup mayonnaise or salad
    dressing
¼ teaspoon garlic salt
¼ teaspoon salt
⅛ teaspoon freshly ground
    black pepper

Drain canned lima beans, or prepare frozen beans according to package directions and drain well. Combine all ingredients. Cover and refrigerate 1 hour or until well chilled.

DUCHESS POTATO SALAD

6 servings　　　　　　　　　　*(photograph on page 175)*

4 medium potatoes
3 eggs
8 slices bacon
1 small can (5.33 fluid
    ounces) PET Evaporated
    Milk
2 tablespoons sugar
2 teaspoons salt
½ teaspoon dry mustard
⅛ teaspoon freshly ground
    black pepper
½ cup chopped green onions
1 cup chopped celery
¼ cup apple cider vinegar

Place potatoes and eggs in 3-quart saucepan and cover with water. Bring water to a boil, reduce heat, and simmer 10 minutes. Remove eggs and place under cold running water to cool. Continue to simmer potatoes an additional 20 to 30 minutes or until tender. When tender, remove from water and allow to cool. Meanwhile, fry bacon until crisp; drain and crumble. Peel and chop eggs. Peel potatoes and slice into medium mixing bowl. Add bacon, eggs, and remaining ingredients to potatoes; gently mix until well blended. Serve warm or chilled.

CREAMY SLAW
Six ½-cup servings

1 small can (5.33 fluid ounces) PET Evaporated Milk
½ cup mayonnaise or salad dressing
¼ cup apple cider vinegar
2 tablespoons sugar
1 teaspoon salt
¼ teaspoon celery seeds
⅛ teaspoon freshly ground black pepper
4 cups shredded cabbage
1 carrot, shredded
1 stalk celery, diced

To form dressing, combine evaporated milk, mayonnaise, vinegar, sugar, salt, celery seed, and pepper. Chill mixture until ready to serve. In serving bowl, combine cabbage, carrot, and celery. Chill until ready to serve. To serve, pour dressing over vegetables; toss to coat. Serve immediately.

RAW VEGETABLE SALAD
8 servings

2 bunches fresh broccoli, cleaned and trimmed
4 firm tomatoes, chopped
1 small red onion, thinly sliced
1 container (½ pint) PET Whipping Cream
⅔ cup vegetable oil
½ cup PET Sour Cream
3 tablespoons red wine vinegar
2 teaspoons prepared mustard
1 teaspoon dillweed
½ teaspoon salt
⅛ teaspoon freshly ground black pepper

Cut off flowerets from broccoli stalks. Peel outer skin from stalks and slice into thin rounds, about ⅛-inch thick. In large bowl, combine broccoli slices and flowerets, tomatoes, and red onion. In separate bowl, combine remaining ingredients; blend well. Pour dressing over vegetables and toss until well coated. Refrigerate salad 1 to 2 hours or until well chilled.

FIESTA CHEESE BURGERS
8 servings

1 1/2 pounds ground beef
1 egg
3/4 cup dry bread crumbs
1 can (4 ounces) OLD EL PASO
     Chopped Green Chilies
1/4 cup OLD EL PASO Taco
     Sauce or OLD EL PASO
     Picante Salsa
1/2 teaspoon salt
8 slices (1 ounce each)
     process American
     cheese
8 hamburger buns

In a bowl, combine ground beef, egg, bread crumbs, green chilies, taco sauce or picante salsa, and salt; mix thoroughly. Shape into 8 patties. Grill over medium coals 8 to 10 minutes. Turn and grill to desired doneness. Add 1 slice of cheese to each patty and cook until melted. Serve on buns. Top burgers with additional taco sauce or picante salsa, if desired.

WESTERN SLAW
Six 1-cup servings

3 hard-cooked eggs
1/3 cup PET Evaporated Milk
3 tablespoons vegetable oil
1 tablespoon sugar
1 1/2 teaspoons salt
3/4 teaspoon dry mustard
1/8 teaspoon freshly
     ground black pepper
3 tablespoons vinegar
4 cups shredded cabbage
1 1/2 cups shredded carrots
3 tablespoons diced
     pimiento
1 tablespoon minced onion

Slice eggs in half to separate yolk and white. Chop egg white and set aside. In small bowl, mash egg yolk with fork. Mix in evaporated milk, oil, sugar, salt, mustard, and pepper. When mixture is well blended, stir in vinegar. Chill dressing until ready to serve. Form slaw by combining egg white, cabbage, carrots, pimiento, and onion. Toss mixture and chill until serving time. At serving time, pour dressing over slaw. Toss mixture until vegetables are lightly coated.

Fiesta Cheese Burgers, Western Slaw

102

COOL SARDINE SANDWICH
4 cool sandwiches

**Butter or margarine,
    softened**
8 slices white bread
**Mayonnaise or salad
    dressing**
16 thin slices cucumber
**2 cans (3³⁄₄ ounces each)
    UNDERWOOD Sardines,
    any variety, chilled
    and well drained**

Butter 4 bread slices and spread mayonnaise on remaining 4 slices. Arrange cucumbers on buttered slices and top with sardines. Press mayonnaise-spread slices firmly on sardines and serve.

OPEN-FACED BACON-SARDINE SANDWICHES
4 sandwiches

**2 cans (3³⁄₄ ounces each)
    UNDERWOOD Sardines,
    any variety, drained**
¹⁄₄ cup lemon juice
¹⁄₂ teaspoon sugar
¹⁄₂ teaspoon salt
**¹⁄₈ teaspoon freshly
    ground black pepper**
4 slices white bread
**Butter or margarine,
    softened**
**6 slices bacon, halved
    and cooked crisp**

Turn sardines out onto shallow plate. Combine lemon juice, sugar, salt, and pepper. Pour over sardines and let stand about 1 hour, basting occasionally. Drain. Place bread slices on baking sheet and toast under broiler on one side only. Butter slices on untoasted side and top each with an equal number of sardines. Top sardines with bacon, allowing 3 half slices per sandwich. Serve immediately.

Good as Gold

Rumors of buried gold lured salvagers to an Iowa cornfield in 1968. No gold was found — but prospectors did turn up something just as interesting. Almost 30 feet below ground lay the rotted hull of the riverboat *Bertrand*, which had sunk in the Missouri River 103 years earlier and had been left buried in dry land by a change in the river's course. Discovered among the well-preserved articles retrieved from the buried vessel were bottles of UNDERWOOD ketchup — examined by scientists and found to be still in sterile condition and loaded with Vitamin C.

FANCY SALAD

Your favorite tossed
   salad mixture
1 can (3³/₄ ounces)
   UNDERWOOD Sardines,
   any variety, drained
   Vinegar

To make any salad special, toss together your family's favorite salad ingredients. Chill salad until ready to serve. About 35 minutes before serving time, place drained sardines in shallow dish. Cover with vinegar. Let stand about 30 minutes. Drain vinegar, and break sardines into bite-size pieces. Top chilled salad with sardine pieces and serve.

NOTE: *Soaking the sardines in vinegar will give them a refreshing taste.*

DEVILED HAM BUNWICHES

4 sandwiches   *(photograph on page 93)*

1 can (4¹/₂ ounces)
   UNDERWOOD Deviled
   Ham
³/₄ cup (3 ounces) shredded
   Cheddar cheese,
   divided usage
4 hamburger buns, lightly
   toasted
¹/₂ cup canned French fried
   onions
4 slices tomato

In small bowl, mix deviled ham and ¼ cup cheese. Spread ham mixture on bottom halves of buns. Top each with French fried onions, 1 tomato slice, and remaining cheese. Place on broiler rack 5 inches from heat and broil until cheese melts. To serve, top sandwiches with bun tops.

CHICKEN CROISSANTS

4 sandwiches

2 cans (4³/₄ ounces each)
   UNDERWOOD Chunky
   Chicken Spread
¹/₄ cup creamy salad dressing
¹/₂ teaspoon coarsely ground
   black pepper
4 croissants or other small
   rolls
   Lettuce leaves
4 tomato slices, halved

In small bowl, mix chicken spread, salad dressing, and pepper. Refrigerate mixture about 1 hour or until well chilled. Cut croissants lengthwise, and line bottom halves with lettuce leaves. Spread chilled chicken mixture over lettuce and top evenly with tomato slices.

104

VANILLA SHAKE

2 servings

1 small can (5.33 fluid
    ounces) PET Evaporated
    Milk, chilled
2/3 cup ice water
1 cup ice
1 tablespoon sugar
1 teaspoon vanilla

Combine all ingredients in blender container. Cover and process on HIGH until smooth and frothy.

THICK STRAWBERRY SHAKE

Four 1-cup servings

2 cups sliced fresh
    strawberries
1 tall can (12 fluid ounces)
    PET Evaporated Milk,
    chilled
1 cup ice
1/4 cup sugar
2 tablespoons lemon juice
1 teaspoon vanilla

Combine all ingredients in blender container. Cover and process on HIGH until smooth and frothy.

CHOCOLATE MILK SHAKE

4 servings

1 cup ice
1 container (1 pint) PET
    Vanilla Ice Cream
1 small can (5.33 fluid
    ounces) PET Evaporated
    Milk
1/2 cup chocolate syrup

Combine all ingredients in blender container. Cover and process on HIGH until smooth and frothy.

ORANGE FROST

2 servings   *(photograph on page 93)*

1 **small can (5.33 fluid
      ounces) PET Evaporated
      Milk, chilled**
²⁄₃ **cup orange juice**
2 **scoops PET Vanilla
      Ice Cream**

Combine all ingredients in blender
container. Cover and process on HIGH until
smooth and frothy.

FRUITY PARFAIT

8 parfaits

2 **pints fresh strawberries,
      washed, hulled, and
      halved**
1 **cup fresh blueberries**
¹⁄₂ **cup sugar**
4 **medium bananas, sliced**
1 **container (¹⁄₂ gallon)
      PET Vanilla Ice Cream,
      softened**
¹⁄₂ **cup pineapple topping**
8 **maraschino cherries**

In large bowl, toss together berries and
sugar. Cover and refrigerate 20 to 30
minutes. Arrange banana slices around
bottoms and sides of 8 parfait glasses.
Layer berries and ice cream alternately in
banana-lined glasses, beginning and
ending with ice cream. Drizzle each with
pineapple topping and top with a cherry.
Serve immediately.

SPRINGTIME LIME SALAD

Eight ¹⁄₂-cup servings

1 **package (3 ounces) lime
      gelatin**
³⁄₄ **cup boiling water**
1 **cup PET Evaporated Milk**
1 **can (8¹⁄₄ ounces) crushed
      pineapple, drained**
¹⁄₂ **cup broken pecans**
1 **cup PET Cottage Cheese**
¹⁄₂ **cup finely chopped celery**
¹⁄₂ **cup mayonnaise or salad
      dressing**
1 **tablespoon lemon juice**

In large mixing bowl, dissolve gelatin in
boiling water. Cool slightly and stir in
evaporated milk. Chill mixture until it is as
thick as unbeaten egg whites. Fold in
remaining ingredients. Pour into 8-inch
square pan or 5-cup mold. Chill until firm.

CREAMY FRUIT CUP

6 fruit cups

1 **carton (8 ounces) PET**
  Swiss Style Yogurt, Plain
1 **can (20 ounces)**
  chilled pineapple
  chunks, drained,
  ¼ cup juice reserved
1 **pint fresh strawberries,**
  washed, hulled, and
  sliced, or 1 package
  (16 ounces) frozen
  sliced strawberries
  drained
1 **container (12 ounces)**
  PET Cottage Cheese

To prepare dressing, mix yogurt and reserved pineapple juice. Cover and refrigerate. In 6 dessert dishes, alternately layer pineapple chunks and strawberry slices, placing cottage cheese between each layer. Refrigerate 1½ to 2 hours or until well chilled. Just before serving, top with yogurt dressing. Serve immediately.

The Ring of Quality

Before manufacturing techniques were perfected, every can of PET Milk was "ear"-tested. Shaking a suspect can close to the ear, a tester could tell by the gurgle whether the can had been improperly sterilized or sealed. For many years Louis Latzer, a founder and early president of Pet, trusted no one else with this final quality test. On one occasion, when a whole carload of milk was in doubt, Latzer stood in his stocking feet for hours, shaking a can in each hand, testing all 40,000 cans.

Creamy Fruit Cup

108

PRALINE PIE

6 to 8 servings

¹/₃ cup butter or margarine
¹/₃ cup firmly packed brown
    sugar
¹/₂ cup chopped pecans
1 PET-RITZ Graham Pie
    Crust Shell
1 package (3⁵/₈ ounces)
    butterscotch pudding
    and pie filling mix
    PET WHIP Non-Dairy
    Whipped Topping,
    thawed

In small saucepan, cook and stir butter and brown sugar over low heat until brown sugar melts and mixture bubbles. Remove from heat and add pecans. Pour into graham crust. Prepare pudding mix according to package directions for pie filling. Cool slightly. Pour over butter and brown sugar mixture. Chill 4 hours or until firm. Just before serving, garnish with PET WHIP.

CREAMY PISTACHIO PIE

6 servings

(photograph on page 93)

1 tall can (12 fluid ounces)
    PET Evaporated Milk,
    chilled
1 package (3³/₄ ounces)
    instant pistachio
    pudding and pie filling
    mix
2 cups PET WHIP Non-Dairy
    Whipped Topping,
    thawed
1 PET-RITZ Regular Pie
    Crust Shell, baked
    Chopped pistachio nuts
    (optional)

Pour cold evaporated milk into small mixing bowl. Add pudding mix. Beat with electric mixer on LOW 2 minutes. Fold in PET WHIP. Pour into baked pie shell. Garnish with chopped nuts if desired. Freeze until firm. Remove from freezer about 15 minutes before serving for ease in cutting.

NOTE: *For a pie with a more puddinglike texture, refrigerate instead of freezing.*

Sugar-Coated Fantasy

Pralines were named for a French diplomat, Cesar du Plessis-Praslin, who fancied sugar-coated almonds. The candies underwent a transformation in Louisiana, where the Creoles substituted their native pecans for almonds and used brown sugar instead of white. The simple confection is sometimes enhanced with cream and molasses.

"BERRIED" TREASURE PIE

6 to 8 servings

1 **package (8 ounces) cream cheese, softened**
2 **tablespoons sugar**
1 **cup plus 2 tablespoons milk, divided usage**
1 **PET-RITZ Deep Dish Pie Crust Shell, baked**
1 **cup sliced strawberries**
1 **package (3³⁄₄ ounces) lemon instant pudding and pie filling mix**
1 **container (8 ounces) PET WHIP Non-Dairy Whipped Topping, thawed, divided usage**

In small bowl, beat cream cheese, sugar, and 2 tablespoons milk until smooth. Spread evenly in bottom of pie crust. Arrange strawberries on cream cheese mixture. Prepare pudding mix with remaining 1 cup milk according to package directions for pie filling. Fold in 1 cup PET WHIP. Pour over strawberries. Chill until firm. Just before serving, garnish with remaining PET WHIP.

STRAWBERRY-BANANA GLAZE PIE

6 to 8 servings

³⁄₄ **cup sugar**
2 **tablespoons cornstarch**
¹⁄₈ **teaspoon salt**
1 **cup water**
1 **tablespoon butter or margarine, softened**
¹⁄₈ **teaspoon red food coloring**
1 **pint strawberries, washed, hulled, and quartered**
2 **bananas, sliced**
1 **PET-RITZ Graham Pie Crust Shell**
PET WHIP Non-Dairy Whipped Topping, thawed

In medium saucepan, combine sugar, cornstarch, and salt. Mix well. Stir in water and butter. Cook over low heat until thickened, stirring constantly. Stir in food coloring. Stir in strawberries. Arrange banana slices on bottom of graham crust. Pour strawberry glaze over bananas. Chill 3 hours. Just before serving, garnish with PET WHIP.

FLUFFY CHEESECAKE

12 servings

- **1 small can (5.33 fluid ounces) PET Evaporated Milk**
- **1 cup graham cracker crumbs**
- **¹/₄ cup butter or margarine, melted**
- **1 package (3 ounces) lemon gelatin**
- **1 cup boiling water**
- **1 package (8 ounces) cream cheese, softened**
- **1 cup sugar**
- **4 tablespoons lemon juice, divided usage**

VARIATIONS:

Nutty Cheesecake: *Before chilling the cake, top with ½ cup chopped nuts.*

Orange Glazed Cheesecake: *Prepare cheesecake as directed. Peel and section 1 large orange. When cake is firm, arrange orange sections on top of cake. Prepare glaze by mixing ¼ cup sugar and 1 tablespoon cornstarch in small saucepan. Add 1 cup strained orange juice. Bring mixture to a boil, and boil 1 minute. Remove from heat and stir in 1 tablespoon butter or margarine and 1 tablespoon lemon juice. Allow mixture to cool slightly. Pour over cake and chill about 1 hour or until firm.*

Step 1: *Pour evaporated milk into small mixing bowl.* Place milk, mixing bowl, and beaters in freezer. Freeze just until ice crystals form along outside edge.

Step 2: Mix graham cracker crumbs and butter. *Press mixture firmly into bottom of 9-inch springform pan* or 11 × 7-inch baking pan.

(continued on page 112)

Orange Glaze Cheesecake

112

Step 3: *Dissolve gelatin in boiling water.* Chill mixture until thick but not firm. In large mixing bowl, cream together cream cheese and sugar until smooth.

Step 4: *Add thickened gelatin and 2 tablespoons lemon juice* to cream cheese mixture; beat thoroughly until well blended.

Step 5: Remove evaporated milk from freezer. Add remaining 2 tablespoons lemon juice. Beat with electric mixer on HIGH until *stiff peaks form.*

Step 6: Gently fold whipped evaporated milk into gelatin mixture. *Pour mixture into graham cracker crumb-lined pan.* Chill until firm.

MOCHA CHOCOLATE ICE CREAM
2 quarts

2 tall cans (12 fluid ounces each) Pet Evaporated Milk, divided usage
2 squares (1 ounce each) WHITMAN'S Unsweetened Baking Chocolate
2 to 3 tablespoons instant coffee granules
2 eggs
1 cup sugar
1 cup chopped pecans or almonds

In small saucepan, combine 1 cup evaporated milk, chocolate, and coffee granules. Cook over medium heat, stirring frequently, until chocolate melts and mixture is smooth. Meanwhile, beat eggs and sugar in large mixing bowl until well blended. Stir in hot chocolate mixture. Stir in remaining evaporated milk. Refrigerate until well chilled. Pour into ice cream freezer container. Churn and freeze according to manufacturer's directions. When ice cream is finished, stir in pecans.

PEANUT BUTTER CHOCOLATE ICE CREAM
2 quarts

2 tall cans (12 fluid ounces each) PET Evaporated Milk, divided usage
2 squares (1 ounce each) WHITMAN'S Unsweetened Baking Chocolate
2 eggs
3/4 cup sugar
4 to 6 tablespoons chunky peanut butter

In small saucepan, combine 1 cup evaporated milk and chocolate. Cook over medium heat, stirring frequently, until chocolate melts and mixture is smooth. Meanwhile, beat eggs and sugar in large mixing bowl until well blended. Beat in peanut butter until smooth. Stir in hot chocolate mixture. Stir in remaining evaporated milk. Refrigerate until well chilled. Pour into ice cream freezer container. Churn and freeze according to manufacturer's directions.

FROZEN FRUIT DELIGHT

12 servings

**1 envelope unflavored
    gelatin
1 can (16 ounces) pineapple
    chunks, drained, 1/2 cup
    juice reserved
1 package (3 ounces) cream
    cheese, softened
1 container (8 ounces)
    PET Sour Cream
1/4 cup sugar
1 can (16 ounces) sliced
    peaches, drained
1 can (11 ounces) mandarin
    oranges, drained
1 cup chopped pecans
1 container (8 ounces)
    PET WHIP Non-Dairy
    Whipped Topping,
    thawed**

In 1½-quart saucepan over low heat, dissolve gelatin in reserved pineapple juice. Remove from heat. In separate bowl, beat cream cheese until smooth. Add sour cream, sugar, and gelatin mixture, mixing well. Stir in pineapple, peaches, mandarin oranges, and pecans. Gently fold in PET WHIP. Pour into 11 × 7-inch dish. Cover tightly and freeze overnight. Remove from freezer and let stand 1 hour at room temperature before serving.

*Pork Stir-Fry (page 116), Hearty Beefy Enchiladas (page 131),
New England Clam Chowder (page 140), B&M Brown Bread*

Go West, Go East, Go South

PORK STIR-FRY

3 to 4 servings   *(photograph on page 115)*

**¹/₂ pound pork tenderloin,
     sliced into thin strips
2 tablespoons vegetable oil
¹/₂ pound broccoli, sliced
¹/₂ pound mushrooms,
     sliced
¹/₂ cup chopped green
     onions
¹/₄ cup water
2 tablespoons soy sauce
1 tablespoon dry sherry
1 tablespoon honey
1 teaspoon cornstarch
¹/₂ teaspoon AC'CENT
     Flavor Enhancer
¹/₈ teaspoon garlic powder
1 can (11 ounces) mandarin
     oranges, drained
2 cups warm cooked rice**

In wok or large skillet, brown sliced meat about 2 to 3 minutes in hot oil. Push meat to side and add broccoli, mushrooms, and green onions; stir-fry vegetables 2 minutes. In separate bowl, combine water, soy sauce, sherry, honey, cornstarch, AC'CENT, and garlic powder; mix thoroughly. Pour soy sauce mixture over vegetables and continue to heat until sauce begins to thicken, stirring constantly. When mixture begins to thicken, quickly stir in mandarin oranges, and heat an additional 30 seconds, just to warm oranges. Serve immediately over warm rice.

Beside the Gateway Arch

A 15-story tower completed in 1968, overlooking an 82-acre park and the rolling waters of the Mississippi, is Pet's home in St. Louis. Outside the tower's windows, soaring 630 feet in the air, is the shining stainless-steel Gateway Arch, which commemorates the Louisiana Purchase and St. Louis' historic role as "Gateway to the West."

ORIENTAL MEATBALL SOUP

4 to 6 servings

1/2 pound ground pork
1 tablespoon soy sauce
2 teaspoons cornstarch
1 teaspoon grated onion
1/2 teaspoon AC'CENT
 Flavor Enhancer
1 egg yolk, beaten
3 cans (14 1/2 ounces each)
 chicken broth,
 divided usage
1/2 cup chopped onions
1/2 cup chopped celery
1 package (10 ounces)
 frozen green peas,
 thawed
1/2 cup thinly sliced
 cabbage

In small bowl, combine pork, soy sauce, cornstarch, grated onion, AC'CENT, and egg yolk. Mix well. Form mixture into marble-size meatballs; refrigerate. In large saucepan, combine 2 cans chicken broth, chopped onions, and celery; bring to a boil. Reduce heat and simmer 10 minutes. Add meatballs to broth mixture; cover and simmer 20 minutes. Add remaining 1 can chicken broth, peas, and cabbage; bring to a boil. Reduce heat and simmer 5 minutes.

SHRIMP FRIED RICE

4 to 6 servings

2 cans (4 1/4 ounces each)
 ORLEANS Deveined
 Medium Shrimp, drained
2 eggs
4 cups cooked long grain
 rice, chilled
1/2 teaspoon AC'CENT
 Flavor Enhancer
1 teaspoon dry sherry
 (optional)
1/3 cup minced onion
2 tablespoons chopped
 pimiento (optional)
1/4 cup vegetable oil
1 cup frozen peas,
 thawed
1/4 cup soy sauce

Rinse shrimp under cold running water. Drain. Scramble eggs over low heat, cooking until firm. Chop scrambled eggs. Place chilled rice in medium bowl. Add AC'CENT, sherry if desired, onion, and pimientos if desired; blend thoroughly. In large skillet or wok, heat oil over medium heat until hot. Pour rice mixture into hot oil and stir-fry 8 minutes. Add drained shrimp and peas; cook an additional 2 minutes. Remove from heat, add chopped egg and soy sauce; mix and serve immediately.

ORIENTAL CHICKEN WONTONS

30 appetizers

**2 cups diced cooked
    chicken
¹/₄ cup minced celery
¹/₄ cup minced water
    chestnuts
¹/₃ cup minced green onion
1 teaspoon cornstarch
¹/₂ teaspoon AC'CENT
    Flavor Enhancer
¹/₂ teaspoon salt
¹/₄ teaspoon dry mustard
1 tablespoon soy sauce
1 teaspoon lemon juice
Wonton wrappers
Oil for deep-fat frying**

In medium bowl, combine all ingredients except wonton wrappers and oil and blend thoroughly. Place 1 teaspoon chicken mixture in center of each wonton wrapper. Dampen edge of wrappers with water and fold in envelope fashion, making sure all edges are sealed. In deep-fat fryer, heat 3 inches of oil to 375°F. Fry chicken envelopes about 2 minutes or until golden brown on both sides. May be served with a sweet-and-sour sauce or hot mustard sauce.

CHICKEN SNOW PEA STIR-FRY

4 servings

**³/₄ pound raw chicken,
    cubed
2 teaspoons cornstarch,
    divided usage
1 tablespoon soy sauce
2 tablespoons vegetable oil
1 medium onion, cut
    into wedges
1 cup Chinese snow peas
¹/₂ cup sliced mushrooms
¹/₂ cup chicken broth
¹/₂ teaspoon AC'CENT
    Flavor Enhancer
2 cups warm cooked rice
Slivered almonds**

In small bowl, combine chicken, 1 teaspoon cornstarch, and soy sauce. In medium skillet or wok, heat oil; stir-fry chicken mixture in hot oil 3 to 5 minutes or until chicken is opaque. Add onion, snow peas, and mushrooms; stir-fry an additional 2 minutes. Combine chicken broth, remaining 1 teaspoon cornstarch and AC'CENT; mix well. Add broth mixture to vegetables and bring to a boil, stirring constantly. Serve immediately over warm rice and garnish with almonds.

Oriental Chicken Wontons, Chicken Snow Pea Stir-Fry

ORIENTAL STEAK STRIPS

4 servings

2 pounds flank or sirloin steak, cut diagonally into strips
1 1/2 tablespoons vegetable oil
1 garlic clove, minced
1 medium green pepper, cut into thin strips
1 can (13.3 ounces) COMPLIMENT Brown Sauce
1/3 cup firmly packed brown sugar
1/3 cup vinegar
1/4 cup soy sauce
1/4 teaspoon ground ginger
Freshly ground black pepper to taste
3 tablespoons cornstarch
1 can (1 pound 4 ounces) pineapple chunks, drained, liquid reserved
2 cups warm cooked rice

In skillet, brown steak strips in hot oil with garlic. In slow cooker on LOW, cook steak strips, green pepper, COMPLIMENT, brown sugar, vinegar, soy sauce, ginger, and pepper 6 to 8 hours (on HIGH cook 4 hours). Mix cornstarch and reserved pineapple liquid and add to sauce. Set slow cooker on HIGH, bring to a boil, stirring frequently until thickened. Five minutes before serving, add pineapple chunks. Serve over a bed of warm rice.

PEPPER STEAK

4 to 6 servings

1 pound beefsteak, sliced into thin strips
2 tablespoons vegetable oil
1 cup sliced celery
1 cup chopped onions
1 cup beef bouillon
1 green pepper, cut into strips
2 tablespoons cornstarch
1/2 teaspoon AC'CENT Flavor Enhancer
3 tablespoons soy sauce
1 tablespoon lemon juice
2 medium tomatoes, cut into wedges
Freshly ground black pepper to taste
3 cups warm cooked rice

In wok or large skillet, brown meat strips in hot oil; meat should remain pink inside. Add celery, onions, and beef bouillon to meat, and toss. Cover mixture and simmer 40 minutes. Add green pepper, cover, and simmer an additional 3 to 5 minutes. In separate bowl, combine cornstarch, AC'CENT, soy sauce, and lemon juice; mix well. Add soy sauce mixture to meat; continue to heat 1 minute or until sauce thickens. Add tomato wedges, and cook an additional 20 seconds to warm tomatoes. Sprinkle mixture with pepper and serve immediately over warm rice.

International

It's a small world, and it seems to be getting smaller when Pet's products turn up on tables in Venezuela, Mexico, Australia, England, Canada, Sweden, Costa Rica, Saudi Arabia, and other exotic lands. For years we've exported some products and produced others in cooperation with foreign firms. Much of our overseas business came to us in 1982 along with the Wm. Underwood Company and its foreign subsidiaries. Those subsidiaries, mainly canners of meat and fish products, each brought to us its own unique and colorful history, and a well-established name and reputation in its own land.

In America, Pet has helped spread the goodness of regional delicacies from coast to coast. Now our International Group introduces American favorites to people in many lands — SEGO diet foods to Saudi Arabia, DOWNYFLAKE waffles to Canada, and OLD EL PASO Mexican foods from the United Kingdom to Japan. And the list keeps growing. It seems that no matter where we go, quality, convenience, and good taste speak a universal language.

Along the Rio Grande, near El Paso, Texas, the canning of green chilies is a major fall industry. The work tempo builds to a furious pace in mid-October just before frost strikes to turn the green chilies red.

In this area, you'll find the largest canner of green chilies — indeed, the country's number one brand of Mexican food — Old El Paso. Fifteen years ago, that name was associated with a small label known only in a few southwestern states. To understand the rich heritage of Old El Paso, you must first know a little about a company called Mountain Pass Canning.

Like many successful American businesses, Mountain Pass started on less than a shoestring. On their farm in New Mexico, a family named

Powell canned tomatoes, and pinto beans in chili sauce — not to sell, but to feed themselves and their farmhands. Neighbors liked the foods and asked to buy them.

In the early 1920s, the Powells sold their farm and moved to Canutillo, Texas, just outside El Paso, where they opened a cannery. Their total output was 20,000 cases a year — not quite a third of what Old El Paso now packs in a single day.

The little company was bought two decades later by three partners who set about enlarging and improving it. Wartime restrictions on canning slowed things down a bit, but the company held its own. Vegetables were its business — beans, spinach, onions — and later green chilies, and tomato and green chili sauces. By the 1950s more Mexican foods were joining the line-up.

Plans were underway to remodel the little cannery in Canutillo when disaster struck — disaster that came as a blessing in disguise. Rio Grande floodwaters deluged the plant, drowning equipment and wiping out thousands of dollars of canned goods. With ripe crops ready for canning, the business needed to get back in business quickly, or lose everything. So negotiations were begun and concluded with dispatch, and a new, larger plant was purchased in nearby Anthony, Texas. That expanded facility is still in use today. The small original plant would never have been adequate for

expanding needs; so thanks to the flood of the Rio Grande, many thousands of renovation dollars were saved.

A few years earlier, Mountain Pass had acquired a competitor, Valley Canning Company, and with it the OLD EL PASO label. Products were distributed under both names until 1968, when Pet purchased the Texas producer of Mexican foods and launched a period of great change and growth.

We at Pet recognized that changing lifestyles signaled a change in eating habits. With the trends toward more casual eating and growing interest in flavor and spice, Americans were discovering Mexican food. We knew the OLD EL PASO name and reputation, and we knew that the company had the potential for tremendous growth with Pet's support. Together we could provide American consumers with the wide variety of Mexican products they craved.

To our customers, the name OLD EL PASO meant quality southwestern Mexican food. So we began a gradual phase-out of the Mountain Pass name, while holding onto the best of the Mountain Pass products — refried beans, taco sauces, green chilies, and other favorites.

Then we began to introduce new products. We'd always sold taco sauce (in fact, our taco sauce is made from a patented formula developed by an employee almost 40 years ago and based on a traditional Mexican recipe); but we switched from cans to glass jars and began to offer our sauce in varieties to suit any taste — from "mild" to "medium" to spicy "hot." Then we came out with OLD EL PASO Taco Shells, Taco Seasoning Mix, NACHIPS Tortilla Chips, Corn Tortillas, and Picante Salsa, a popular sauce with chunks of fresh vegetables. Today, we offer nearly 80 items in six major product categories — sauces and seasonings, shells, beans, chilies, dinners, and tortilla chips. Our new line of frozen entrées satisfies the growing consumer need for Mexican food that's both tasty and quick.

America's appetite has been whetted for convenient high-quality Mexican food, and in satisfying that appetite OLD EL PASO is the number one brand. People are sampling delicious dishes in the many Mexican restaurants springing up around the country and are beginning to experiment with interesting new Mexican foods — burritos, chimichangas, salsa — at home. In fact, the regional favorites of the Southwest and all the wonderful tastes of good Mexican food are today as much at home in kitchens in the Northeast, on the West Coast — all across America — as they are in El Paso, and along the Rio Grande.

TACO SALAD SUPREME
4 to 6 servings

1 pound lean ground beef
1 package (1 1/4 ounces)
OLD EL PASO Taco
Seasoning
1 small head lettuce,
torn into bite-size
pieces (3 to 4 cups)
1 cup (4 ounces) shredded
sharp Cheddar cheese
1/2 cup sliced ripe olives
1 large tomato, cut into
wedges
1 small onion, thinly
sliced and separated
into rings
1 can (15 ounces)
OLD EL PASO Garbanzos,
drained
Avocado slices
Coarsely crushed OLD
EL PASO Taco Shells,
Tostado Shells, or
NACHIPS Tortilla Chips
OLD EL PASO Taco Sauce

Prepare ground beef according to directions on taco seasoning package. In salad bowl, combine lettuce, cheese, and olives; toss well. Top with prepared meat mixture, tomato, onion, garbanzos, avocado slices, and broken shells. Serve with taco sauce.

QUESADILLAS
6 quesadillas

2 cans (4 ounces each)
OLD EL PASO Whole
Green Chilies
8 ounces Cheddar or
Monterey Jack cheese
6 flour tortillas, 8-inch
Oil for frying
OLD EL PASO Taco Sauce
or OLD EL PASO Picante
Salsa

Slit chilies lengthwise. Remove seeds and ribs. Cut cheese into six 4 × 1/2 × 1/2-inch pieces. Wrap each piece of cheese in a chili. Place 1 cheese-filled chili in center of each tortilla. Fold tortillas in half over chili and secure with toothpicks. Fry in one inch of hot oil until crisp, turning occasionally. Drain on paper towels. Serve immediately with taco sauce or picante salsa.

Taco Salad Supreme

BEEF TACOS
12 tacos   *(photograph on page 199)*

1 pound lean ground beef
1 medium onion, chopped
1 garlic clove, minced
1 package (1 1/4 ounces)
   OLD EL PASO Taco
   Seasoning
3/4 cup water
12 OLD EL PASO Taco
   Shells
2 tomatoes, chopped
1 cup (4 ounces) shredded
   sharp Cheddar cheese
Shredded lettuce
OLD EL PASO Taco Sauce

In medium skillet, brown ground beef, onion, and garlic. Drain fat. Stir in taco seasoning and water. Bring to a boil. Reduce heat and simmer, uncovered, 15 to 20 minutes, stirring occasionally. Preheat oven to 350°F. Arrange taco shells on cookie sheet. Warm shells in oven 5 to 7 minutes. Fill each of the taco shells with some of the meat mixture, and top with tomatoes, cheese, and lettuce. Serve with taco sauce.

SOFT TACOS
18 tacos

1 1/2 pounds lean ground
   beef
2 packages (1 1/4 ounces
   each) OLD EL PASO
   Taco Seasoning
1 cup water
1 can (10 3/4 ounces) cream of
   mushroom soup
1 can (10 3/4 ounces)
   tomato soup
1 can (10 ounces)
   OLD EL PASO
   Enchilada Sauce
18 OLD EL PASO Taco
   Shells
1 cup (4 ounces) shredded
   Cheddar cheese

In skillet, brown ground beef. Drain fat. Add taco seasoning and water. Stir. Bring to a boil, reduce heat, and simmer, uncovered, 15 to 20 minutes, stirring occasionally, until liquid is reduced. Preheat oven to 350°F. Combine soups and enchilada sauce. Spoon meat mixture into taco shells. Arrange shells in two 9-inch square baking pans in upright position by leaning them against each other. Pour combined sauces over shells evenly. Sprinkle with cheese. Bake 15 minutes.

CHIMICHANGAS

12 chimichangas

1 pound lean ground beef
1 can (10 ounces)
**   OLD EL PASO Tomatoes**
**   and Green Chilies**
1 package (1¼ ounces)
**   OLD EL PASO Taco**
**   Seasoning**
12 flour tortillas,
**   8-inch**
**   Vegetable oil**
3 cups shredded lettuce
3 cups (12 ounces)
**   shredded Cheddar cheese**
¼ cup sliced green onion
1½ cups OLD EL PASO Taco
**   Sauce or OLD**
**   EL PASO Picante**
**   Salsa**

In medium skillet, brown ground beef. Drain fat. Stir in tomatoes and green chilies and taco seasoning. Simmer 5 minutes. Spoon ¼ cup meat mixture along one edge of 1 tortilla. Fold nearest side over to cover filling. Fold in both edges, envelope fashion. Roll and secure with a toothpick. Repeat with remaining meat mixture and tortillas. Fry in one inch of hot oil until golden, turning as necessary. Drain on paper towels. Keep fried chimichangas warm while preparing others. Before serving, top each chimichanga with ¼ cup lettuce, ¼ cup cheese, 1 teaspoon green onion, and 2 tablespoons taco sauce or picante salsa. Serve immediately.

NOTE: *To keep fried chimichangas warm until serving, hold in oven at 170°F.*

Chimichangas are a variation of burritos that are fried rather than baked.

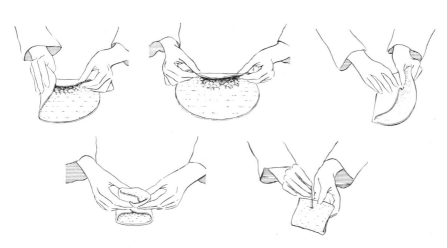

MEXICAN LASAGNA

6 to 8 servings

1 pound lean ground beef
¹/₂ cup chopped onions
1 can (15 ounces) OLD
  EL PASO Mexe-Beans
1 can (8 ounces) tomato
  sauce
1 can (4 ounces)
  OLD EL PASO Chopped
  Green Chilies
1 package (1 ¹/₄ ounces)
  OLD EL PASO Taco
  Seasoning
6 flour tortillas,
  8-inch, halved
2 cups (8 ounces) shredded
  Cheddar cheese

Preheat oven to 350°F. In large skillet, brown ground beef and onions. Drain fat. Stir in mexe-beans, tomato sauce, green chilies, and taco seasoning. Layer half the tortillas on bottom of 11 × 7-inch baking dish. Spread half the meat mixture over, and sprinkle with half the cheese. Repeat layers. Bake 30 minutes. Let stand 10 minutes before serving.

MICROWAVE DIRECTIONS: *Microwave on HIGH 16 to 18 minutes or until heated through. Turn 3 or 4 times during cooking time.*

CHILIES RELLENOS

6 chilies rellenos

6 OLD EL PASO Whole
  Green Chilies
8 ounces Cheddar cheese
6 tablespoons all-purpose
  flour, divided usage
6 eggs, separated
¹/₄ teaspoon salt
  Shortening or oil for
  deep-fat frying
  OLD EL PASO Taco Sauce
  or OLD EL PASO Picante
  Salsa

Slit chilies lengthwise; remove seeds and ribs, and drain on paper towel. Cut cheese into six 3 × ½ × ½-inch strips. Stuff chilies with cheese; roll in 3 tablespoons flour. In medium mixing bowl, beat egg whites until stiff but not dry. Set aside. Add remaining 3 tablespoons flour and salt to egg yolks; beat until thick and lemon-colored. Fold into egg whites. Dip chilies in egg batter, covering well. In deep-fat fryer, heat oil to 400°F. Fry chilies until golden brown all over. Drain on paper towels. Serve immediately with taco sauce or picante salsa.

Mexican Lasagna

SEVICHE

4 to 6 servings

**1 pound scallops, cut
      into small cubes
Lime or lemon juice
1 medium tomato, diced
1/2 medium onion, sliced
      and separated into rings
1 can (4 ounces)
      OLD EL PASO Chopped
      Green Chilies
3 tablespoons vegetable oil
2 tablespoons vinegar
1 tablespoon ground
      coriander
Salt to taste**

In glass or porcelain bowl, cover scallops with lime or lemon juice. Marinate in refrigerator at least 5 hours or overnight. Turn once or twice to be sure that all surfaces are "cooked" by the citrus juice. Turn scallops into colander; drain. Rinse lightly with cold water but not enough to wash out juice. Return scallops to bowl. Add tomato, onion, green chilies, oil, vinegar, coriander, and salt. Mix gently. Serve chilled.

This is a classic Mexican dish, in which the scallops "cook" in the lime or lemon juice.

ENCHILADAS SUIZA

12 enchiladas

**3 cups shredded cooked
      chicken
1 can (4 ounces)
      OLD EL PASO Chopped
      Green Chilies
1 teaspoon salt
1 can (10 ounces) OLD
      EL PASO Green Chili
      Enchilada Sauce
1 small can (5.33 fluid
      ounces) PET Evaporated
      Milk
12 OLD EL PASO Corn
      Tortillas
Vegetable oil
2 cups (8 ounces) shredded
      Monterey Jack cheese**

Preheat oven to 425°F. Mix chicken, green chilies, and salt. In separate bowl, combine enchilada sauce and evaporated milk. Fry tortillas in small amount of hot oil a few seconds on each side to soften. Drain on paper towels. Dip each tortilla in enchilada sauce mixture; fill with ¼ cup chicken mixture; roll and place seam-side down in 13 × 9-inch baking dish. Pour remaining sauce over enchiladas. Sprinkle with cheese. Bake 15 minutes or until bubbly.

MICROWAVE DIRECTIONS: *Microwave, uncovered, on HIGH 8 to 12 minutes or until heated through. Turn once during cooking time.*

SOUTH OF THE BORDER ENCHILADAS
12 enchiladas

1 1/2 pounds lean ground beef
1 package (1 1/4 ounces) OLD EL PASO Taco Seasoning
1 can (12 ounces) tomato paste
1 cup water
1/2 cup chopped onion
1 teaspoon salt
12 flour tortillas, 8-inch
1 jar (8 ounces) pasteurized process cheese spread
1 can (4 ounces) OLD EL PASO Chopped Green Chilies

In large skillet, brown ground beef. Drain well. Stir in taco seasoning, tomato paste, water, onions, and salt. Simmer 15 to 20 minutes, stirring occasionally, until liquid is reduced. Preheat oven to 350°F. Spoon 2 to 3 tablespoons meat mixture on each tortilla. Roll tightly and place in greased 13 × 9-inch baking dish, seam-side down. Spread cheese over top of enchiladas. Sprinkle with green chilies. Top with remaining meat mixture. Bake 25 to 30 minutes. Serve Immediately.

MICROWAVE DIRECTIONS: *Microwave on HIGH 10 to 12 minutes or until heated through. Turn once during cooking time.*

HEARTY BEEFY ENCHILADAS
6 servings   *(photograph on page 115)*

1 1/2 cups shredded cooked beef
3/4 cup chopped onions
2 cups (8 ounces) shredded sharp Cheddar cheese, divided usage
1 can (4 ounces) OLD EL PASO Chopped Green Chilies
1 can (10 3/4 ounces) cream of mushroom soup
1 can (10 3/4 ounces) tomato soup
1 can (10 ounces) OLD EL PASO Enchilada Sauce
12 OLD EL PASO Corn Tortillas
Oil for frying

Combine beef, onions, ½ cup cheese, and green chiles; set aside. To prepare sauce, combine soups and enchilada sauce; set aside. Fry tortillas in ½ inch of hot oil a few seconds on each side to soften. Drain on paper towels. Preheat oven to 350°F. Place 1 heaping tablespoon meat mixture on one end of each tortilla. Roll tortilla and place seam-side down in 13 × 9-inch baking dish. Pour sauce over and top with remaining 1½ cups cheese. Bake 25 to 30 minutes.

MICROWAVE DIRECTIONS: *Microwave enchiladas on 70% POWER 14 to 16 minutes or until heated through. Turn twice during cooking time.*

FLAUTAS

12 flautas, 2 to 3 per serving

1 pound lean ground beef
**1 package (1 ¼ ounces)
     OLD EL PASO Taco
     Seasoning**
**1 jar (16 ounces)
     OLD EL PASO Taco
     Sauce, divided usage**
**24 OLD EL PASO Corn
     Tortillas or flour
     tortillas**
Vegetable oil
**Green onion slivers
     (optional)**

In medium skillet, brown ground beef. Drain fat. Stir in taco seasoning and 1 cup taco sauce. Simmer, uncovered, 5 minutes. Lay 2 tortillas flat and overlapping about 2 inches. Spoon 1 to 2 tablespoons meat filling lengthwise near edge of overlapping tortillas. Roll tortillas tightly around filling and secure with toothpicks. Repeat with remaining meat mixture and tortillas. Fry in one inch of hot oil until flautas are crisp. Drain on paper towels. Serve immediately with remaining taco sauce. Garnish with slivered green onion if desired.

NOTE: *If you are using corn tortillas, the tortillas must be fried in hot oil a few seconds on each side to soften. Drain tortillas on paper towels.*

Flauta means "flute" in Spanish. Flautas are simply tortillas rolled around spicy meat filling and fried crisp.

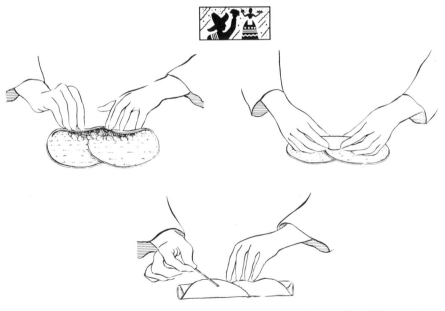

Flautas with OLD EL PASO Taco Sauce

MEXICAN CORN BREAD
6 to 8 servings

2 packages (8 1/2 ounces each) corn muffin mix
2 cans (4 ounces each) OLD EL PASO Chopped Green Chilies, well drained

Preheat oven to 400°F. Prepare corn muffin mix according to package directions. Stir in green chilies. Pour into greased 9-inch square baking pan. Bake 15 to 20 minutes.

NOTE: *Batter may be poured into muffin tins and baked as above. For fewer servings, you can use 1 package of corn muffin mix and 1 can green chilies.*

RUM FLAN
6 to 8 servings

1 1/4 cups sugar, divided usage
4 eggs
2 cups PET Evaporated Milk
2 cups whole milk
2 tablespoons dark rum or 1 tablespoon rum flavoring
1/4 teaspoon salt

Preheat oven to 350°F. In skillet, cook 1/2 cup sugar over low heat, watching carefully. Allow sugar to melt and turn brown (caramelize). Pour caramelized sugar in flan pan (or 2-quart casserole, or soufflé dish). Rotate until bottom is covered. In large mixing bowl, beat eggs and remaining 3/4 cup sugar. Add evaporated milk, whole milk, rum or rum flavoring, and salt. Mix well. Pour milk mixture over caramelized sugar. Place flan pan in large baking pan. Pour warm water into large pan halfway up sides of flan pan. Bake 1 hour 45 minutes to 2 hours or until knife inserted halfway into flan comes out clean (do not pierce bottom). Chill several hours. Unmold.

TOASTED BANANAS
12 servings

6 large firm ripe bananas
3 tablespoons lemon juice
12 flour tortillas, 8-inch
⅔ cup sugar
1 teaspoon ground
cinnamon
⅛ teaspoon ground nutmeg
¼ cup PET Evaporated Milk

Preheat oven to 400°F. Peel bananas and cut in half lengthwise; dip in lemon juice. Place each half at one end of 1 tortilla. Stir together sugar, cinnamon, and nutmeg; sprinkle over bananas, reserving a small amount for top. Roll each tortilla and secure with toothpicks. Brush tortilla lightly with evaporated milk and sprinkle with remaining sugar mixture. Place on well-greased cookie sheet and bake 15 minutes. Remove from cookie sheet immediately. Serve with Orange Sauce or Chocolate Sauce.

ORANGE SAUCE

¼ cup sugar
1 tablespoon cornstarch
1 cup orange juice
1 tablespoon butter
1 tablespoon lemon juice

Mix sugar and cornstarch; add orange juice, and cook, stirring until thickened. Stir in butter and lemon juice. Serve warm over bananas.

CHOCOLATE SAUCE

1 bar (8 ounces) milk
chocolate
1 small can (5.33 fluid
ounces) PET Evaporated
Milk
Pinch salt
1 teaspoon vanilla

In double boiler, melt chocolate. Add evaporated milk and salt. Cook, stirring constantly, about 10 minutes or until slightly thickened. Stir in vanilla. Serve warm over bananas.

TEXAS ORANGE SPICE PECANS
Approximately 4½ cups

1 **cup sugar**
1 **small can (5.33 fluid
    ounces) PET Evaporated
    Milk**
1 **teaspoon ground
    cinnamon**
1 **teaspoon grated
    orange peel
    Dash allspice, ground
    cloves, and salt**
4 **cups pecan halves**

In small saucepan, heat sugar, evaporated milk, and seasonings to soft ball stage (234°F). Remove from heat and add pecans, stirring until mixture begins to thicken and becomes sugary. Spread coated pecans on waxed paper to one layer of thickness. Let cool.

GREEK 'N' CHEESE QUICHE
6 servings

¼ **cup all-purpose flour**
½ **teaspoon salt**
¼ **teaspoon freshly ground
    black pepper**
⅛ **teaspoon marjoram**
1 **large tomato, cut
    into ½-inch slices**
2 **tablespoons vegetable oil**
1 **egg**
¾ **cup PET Whipping
    Cream**
½ **cup (2 ounces) shredded
    Cheddar cheese**
1 **can (2 ounces) sliced
    ripe olives, drained**
¼ **cup chopped green
    onions**
1 **PET-RITZ Regular Pie
    Crust Shell**

Preheat oven and cookie sheet to 375°F. In small bowl, combine flour, salt, pepper, and marjoram. Dip tomato slices in flour mixture, shaking off excess. In large skillet, heat oil over medium-high heat. Add tomatoes to skillet and panfry about 3 minutes or until golden, turning once. Drain well on paper towels. In small bowl, beat eggs lightly. Stir in cream and cheese. Arrange olives, green onions, and tomatoes in pie crust. Pour egg mixture over top. Bake on preheated cookie sheet about 40 minutes or until center is set. Cool 10 minutes before serving.

LOUISIANA CREAM PRALINES

3 dozen candies

**2 cups firmly packed
   brown sugar**
¹/₈ teaspoon salt
³/₄ cup PET Evaporated Milk
**1 tablespoon butter or
   margarine**
2 cups pecan halves

In 2-quart saucepan, mix brown sugar, salt, evaporated milk, and butter. Cook mixture over low heat until brown sugar is dissolved, stirring constantly. Continue to stir, and add pecans; cook over medium heat to soft ball stage (234°F). Remove from heat and allow mixture to cool 5 minutes. Stir cooled mixture until it begins to thicken and coat pecans lightly. Drop quickly by teaspoonfuls onto aluminum foil or lightly buttered cookie sheet. Cool candy until set.

SPOON BREAD

8 servings

1 cup cornmeal
**1 tall can (12 fluid ounces)
   PET Evaporated Milk,
   divided usage**
1 cup water
3 eggs, separated
2 tablespoons shortening
1 teaspoon baking powder
1 teaspoon salt

Preheat oven to 325°F. In 2-quart saucepan, mix cornmeal, 1 cup evaporated milk, and water. Cook, stirring constantly, over medium heat until mixture becomes very thick. Remove from heat and stir in slightly beaten egg yolks, remaining evaporated milk, shortening, baking powder, and salt, stirring until smooth. In separate bowl, beat egg whites until soft peaks form. Fold beaten egg whites into cornmeal mixture. Pour into greased 2-quart casserole. Bake 50 to 55 minutes. Serve immediately.

NOTE: *Spoon bread makes a nice change-of-pace substitute for potatoes or rice. It must be served immediately. As bread cools, it will lose volume.*

SHRIMP JAMBALAYA

4 servings

1 can (4¹/₄ ounces)
    ORLEANS Deveined
    Medium Shrimp
3 tablespoons vegetable oil
³/₄ cup (¹/₄ pound) cubed
    lean ham
¹/₄ cup chopped green
    pepper
2 tablespoons diced onion
1¹/₂ cups water
1¹/₄ cups uncooked rice
1 can (14¹/₂ ounces)
    tomatoes, chopped
1 bay leaf
¹/₄ teaspoon thyme
1 garlic clove, sliced
1 to 2 dashes cayenne
    pepper

Drain shrimp, reserving liquid. In heavy pan, heat oil, and sauté ham, green pepper, and onion about 2 minutes. Add water, rice, tomatoes, and seasonings. Boil, uncovered, 5 minutes, stirring occasionally. Remove from heat. Add shrimp and reserved liquid; toss lightly with fork to mix. Cover tightly and simmer 15 minutes or until rice is tender and all liquid is absorbed. Remove bay leaf before serving.

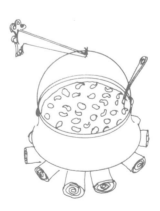

Creole Classic

The Spanish introduced jambalaya to New Orleans in the late 18th century, naming the spicy dish after their word for ham, *jamon*. Jambalaya was made only with ham at first, but Creole cooks added shrimp and turned it into one of their own classic dishes. Now jambalaya may be made with crab, shrimp, chicken, ham, or a combination of all.

140

PLYMOUTH BAKED BEAN SOUP
Six 1-cup servings

3 slices bacon
1 cup diced ham
¼ cup chopped onion
¼ cup chopped green
**   pepper**
¼ cup chopped celery
1 can (28 ounces) B&M
**   Brick Oven Baked Beans**
**   (salt pork removed)**
1 can (1 pound) tomatoes,
**   cut into small pieces,**
**   liquid reserved**
½ cup water
1 tablespoon vinegar
2 teaspoons brown sugar
½ teaspoon salt
** B&M Brown Bread, Plain**
**   or with Raisins**
**   (optional)**

Cook bacon until crisp. Drain and reserve 2 tablespoons drippings. In medium saucepan, sauté ham, onion, green pepper, and celery in reserved drippings. Add beans, tomatoes and liquid, water, vinegar, brown sugar, and salt. Cover and simmer 30 minutes. Serve hot soup garnished with crumbled bacon. Serve with B&M Brown Bread, if desired.

NEW ENGLAND CLAM CHOWDER
4 servings   *(photograph on page 115)*

3 slices bacon
1 small onion, finely
**   chopped**
¼ cup finely chopped
**   celery**
2 cans (6½ ounces each)
**   minced clams**
1½ cups diced potatoes
½ teaspoon salt
1 tall can (12 fluid ounces)
**   PET Evaporated Milk**
** B&M Boston Brown Bread**
**   (optional)**

In medium saucepan, cook bacon until crisp. Drain fat, reserving 1 tablespoon. Crumble bacon and return with reserved fat to saucepan. Stir in onion and celery, cooking until tender. Drain liquid from clams into measuring cup. If needed, add enough water to clam juice to make 1 cup liquid. Stir liquid into onion mixture. Add potatoes and salt. Heat mixture until it begins to boil. Reduce heat, cover, and simmer 20 minutes or until potatoes are tender. Add clams and evaporated milk. Heat until steaming, but do not boil. Serve immediately with Boston brown bread if desired.

Pumpkin Pie with PET WHIP Non-Dairy Whipped Topping (page 156), Famous Creamy Marshmallow Fudge (page 163), Italiano Meat Pie (page 143), Chicken Chilies Rellenos with OLD EL PASO Picante Salsa (page 142)

The People's Choice

142

HEARTY FRENCH ONION SOUP
Four 1-cup servings

¼ cup butter or margarine
2 medium onions, sliced
2 cans (13.3 ounces each)
    COMPLIMENT Brown
    Sauce
4 slices French bread
1 cup (4 ounces) shredded
    Swiss cheese

In 2-quart saucepan, melt butter. Stir in onions. Cook until onions are translucent and slightly browned. Stir in brown sauce and heat to a boil. Reduce heat and simmer. When ready to serve, ladle into ovenproof bowls, and top with bread and cheese. Brown cheese under broiler. Serve immediately.

CHICKEN CHILIES RELLENOS
6 chicken chilies rellenos   *(photograph on page 141)*

3 boneless chicken
    breasts, halved, skin
    removed
1 can (10 ounces)
    OLD EL PASO Whole
    Green Chilies
8 ounces Monterey Jack or
    Cheddar cheese
2 cups all-purpose flour
2 teaspoons salt
1 teaspoon freshly ground
    black pepper
½ teaspoon paprika
2 eggs
½ cup milk
    Oil for deep-fat frying
    OLD EL PASO Taco Sauce
    or OLD EL PASO Picante
    Salsa

Flatten chicken breasts with meat mallet. Slit chilies, lengthwise, removing seeds and ribs. Place 1 chili on each chicken breast. Cut cheese into six 3 × ½ × ½-inch strips. Place 1 piece of cheese on 1 end of a chili and roll up chicken breast jelly-roll fashion. Secure with toothpicks. Repeat with remaining chicken breasts. Season flour with salt, pepper, and paprika. Beat together eggs and milk. Dip each chicken roll in egg, then flour. Repeat. Deep-fat fry at 400°F 10 minutes or until golden brown. Drain on paper towels. Serve with taco sauce or picante salsa.

This recipe is both a consumer favorite and a favorite of PET employees. As an employee favorite, the dish is served at numerous luncheons.

TORTILLA SOUP

4 servings

2 to 3 OLD EL PASO Corn Tortillas
Oil for frying
2 teaspoons vegetable oil
1/3 cup chopped onion
4 cups chicken broth
1 cup shredded cooked chicken
1 can (10 ounces) OLD EL PASO Tomatoes and Green Chilies
1 can (4 ounces) OLD EL PASO Chopped Green Chilies
Salt to taste
1 tablespoon lime juice
4 large lime slices

Cut tortillas into 2 × ½-inch strips. Fry tortillas in small amount of hot oil until brown and crisp. Drain on paper towels. In large saucepan, heat 2 teaspoons vegetable oil. Add onion and sauté until translucent. Add broth, chicken, tomatoes and green chilies, green chilies, and salt. Cover and simmer 20 minutes. Stir in lime juice. To serve, pour into 4 soup bowls and add tortilla strips. Float 1 lime slice in center of each bowl.

ITALIANO MEAT PIE

6 servings

(photograph on page 141)

1 PET-RITZ Deep Dish Pie Crust Shell
1 1/2 pounds lean ground beef
1/3 cup chopped green pepper
2 cans (8 ounces each) tomato sauce
1 can (4 ounces) mushroom stems and pieces, drained
3 tablespoons water
1/4 teaspoon oregano
1/4 teaspoon basil
1/4 teaspoon garlic powder
1/3 cup Parmesan cheese
2 cups (8 ounces) shredded Mozzarella cheese, divided usage

Preheat oven and cookie sheet to 400°F. In large skillet, brown beef. Drain well. Add green pepper and cook 2 minutes. Stir in tomato sauce, mushrooms, water, oregano, basil, and garlic powder. Simmer 10 minutes. Sprinkle half the Parmesan cheese over bottom of pie crust. Spread half the beef mixture over Parmesan cheese. Sprinkle with 1 cup Mozzarella cheese. Layer remaining beef and Parmesan cheese. Bake on preheated cookie sheet 25 minutes. Sprinkle with remaining 1 cup Mozzarella cheese. Return to oven 5 minutes or until cheese melts. Let stand 10 minutes before serving.

TEXAS STYLE NACHOS
6 to 8 servings

**1 cup (8 ounces)
    pasteurized process
    cheese spread**
**1 box (7 1/2 ounces)
    OLD EL PASO NACHIPS
    Tortilla Chips**
**1 can (4 ounces) OLD
    EL PASO Chopped Green
    Chilies, drained**
**OLD EL PASO Taco Sauce
    or OLD EL PASO Picante
    Salsa (optional)**
PET Sour Cream
Guacamole (page 201)

Heat cheese spread. On serving dish, layer half the tortilla chips, green chilies, and process cheese spread. Repeat layers. Top with taco sauce or picante salsa if desired. Serve with sour cream and guacamole.

MICROWAVE DIRECTIONS: *In small microwave safe bowl, microwave cheese spread on 50% POWER 4 minutes or until melted. Stir after 2 minutes.*

GAZPACHO SALAD
4 to 6 servings

**4 medium tomatoes,
    chopped**
**1 cup OLD EL PASO Taco
    Sauce or OLD EL PASO
    Picante Salsa**
**1 cup chopped cucumber
    (1/4-inch cubes)**
1/4 cup olive oil
2 tablespoons basil
**2 tablespoons sherry or
    red wine vinegar**
**2 tablespoons chopped
    red onion**
**2 tablespoons chopped
    green onion**
**2 tablespoons OLD EL PASO
    Chopped Green Chilies**
**2 garlic cloves, finely
    minced**
**1/4 teaspoon ground
    coriander**
**Salt and freshly ground
    black pepper**
**OLD EL PASO NACHIPS
    Tortilla Chips**

In bowl, combine all ingredients except NACHIPS Tortilla Chips. Quantities of various ingredients may be varied according to taste. Chill. Serve with chips.

Texas Style Nachos with PET Sour Cream and Guacamole (page 201), Gazpacho Salad

CAULIFLOWER QUICHE
6 servings

1 ½ **cups (6 ounces) shredded Cheddar cheese**
1 **package (10 ounces) frozen cauliflower, thawed, drained, and sliced**
½ **cup chopped green pepper**
¼ **cup chopped onion**
2 **tablespoons all-purpose flour**
1 **PET-RITZ Deep Dish Pie Crust Shell**
3 **eggs, slightly beaten**
1 **cup milk**
1 **teaspoon salt**
¼ **teaspoon freshly ground black pepper**

Preheat oven and cookie sheet to 400°F. In medium mixing bowl, combine cheese, cauliflower, green pepper, and onion. Sprinkle with flour and toss lightly. Pour into pie crust. In small bowl, mix eggs, milk, salt, and pepper. Pour over cauliflower mixture. Bake on preheated cookie sheet 35 to 40 minutes or until knife inserted comes out clean. Cool 10 minutes before serving.

HAM AND HERB VEGETABLE DIP
1⅔ cups

1 **package (8 ounces) cream cheese, softened**
1 **can (2¼ ounces) UNDERWOOD Deviled Ham**
¼ **cup mayonnaise or salad dressing**
¼ **cup PET Evaporated Milk**
2 **tablespoons diced onion**
1 **tablespoon parsley flakes**
¼ **teaspoon dillweed**
¼ **teaspoon garlic powder**
4 **drops hot pepper sauce**

In small bowl, combine all ingredients. Beat until smooth and creamy. Refrigerate 1 to 2 hours or until well chilled.

COTTAGE ENCHILADAS
6 servings

4 cups (16 ounces) shredded sharp American cheese, divided usage
1 carton (12 ounces) PET Cottage Cheese
2 cans (4 ounces each) OLD EL PASO Chopped Green Chilies
1 garlic clove, minced
1/2 teaspoon ground coriander
1/2 teaspoon salt
1/8 teaspoon freshly ground black pepper
12 OLD EL PASO Corn Tortillas, or flour tortillas, 6-inch or 8-inch
Oil for frying
1 cup PET Sour Cream
1 can (10 ounces) OLD EL PASO Green Chili Enchilada Sauce

Preheat oven to 350°F. Mix 2 cups American cheese, cottage cheese, green chilies, garlic, coriander, salt, and pepper. Set aside. If using flour tortillas, eliminate frying stage. Fry corn tortillas in hot oil a few seconds on each side to soften. Drain on paper towels. Spoon 1 heaping tablespoon cheese mixture on each tortilla. Roll, and place seam-side down in 13 × 9-inch baking dish. Spoon remaining cheese mixture in a row over center of enchiladas. Combine sour cream and enchilada sauce. Pour over tortillas. Top with remaining shredded cheese. Bake 25 to 30 minutes or until bubbly.

MICROWAVE DIRECTIONS: *Microwave enchiladas at 70% POWER 14 to 16 minutes or until heated through. Turn twice during cooking time.*

New-Fangled Food
Preserved meats were an unexpected shipboard treat for one forty-niner who sailed from Massachusetts to San Francisco en route to the gold fields. Until Underwood came along, standard fare on such a long voyage was likely to be dried, pickled, or salt-cured meat. But "preserved meats," the prospector wrote home, ". . . are put up in two-pound tin canisters, the air all pumped out of them and soldered up tight, and it will keep a great many years in any climate. They are bought at Underwood and Co., Boston."

148

SHRIMP NEWBURG
6 servings

**3 cans (4¼ ounces each)
ORLEANS Deveined
Medium or Small Shrimp**
¼ cup butter or margarine
**2½ tablespoons all-purpose
flour**
**2 containers (½ pint each)
PET Light Cream**
¾ teaspoon salt
Dash ground nutmeg
Dash cayenne pepper
2 egg yolks, beaten
**2 tablespoons sherry
(optional)**
**6 slices bread, toasted, or
6 puff pastry shells,
baked**

Step 1: Rinse shrimp under cold running water. Drain. In small saucepan, melt butter; *blend in flour* to make a paste.

Step 2: S*tir in cream*, salt, nutmeg, and cayenne pepper, and cook over medium heat until thick and smooth.

Step 3: Stir ½ *cup of the heated sauce into beaten egg yolks* to warm them.

(continued on page 150)

Shrimp Newburg

150

Step 4: Then *pour yolk mixture into sauce,* stirring constantly.

Step 5: *Add shrimp* and heat until steaming. Remove from heat and slowly stir in sherry if desired. Serve immediately on toast or in puff pastry shells.

BASIC WHITE SAUCE
1 cup

2 tablespoons butter or margarine
2 tablespoons all-purpose flour
¹/₄ teaspoon salt
  Dash black pepper
¹/₂ cup PET Evaporated Milk
¹/₂ cup water

In saucepan, melt butter over medium heat. Add flour, salt, and pepper; mix well. Add evaporated milk and water all at once. Continue to cook over medium heat until mixture boils. Boil 1 additional minute or until thick.

RICH AND CREAMY MUSHROOM SAUCE
2 cups

¼ cup butter or margarine
2 cups sliced fresh
    mushrooms
¼ cup minced green onions
½ teaspoon salt
⅛ teaspoon ground nutmeg
1 container (8 ounces)
    PET Sour Cream

In medium skillet, melt butter over medium heat. Add mushrooms, green onions, salt, and nutmeg. Sauté vegetables until tender. Stir in sour cream. Heat through but do not boil. Use as a sauce over steaks, potatoes, or noodles.

CHEESY MACARONI
6 servings

2 cups elbow macaroni
1½ cups (6 ounces)
    shredded Cheddar
    cheese, divided
    usage
1 tall can (12 fluid ounces)
    PET Evaporated Milk
1 teaspoon dry mustard
1 teaspoon salt
¼ teaspoon freshly ground
    black pepper

Preheat oven to 350°F. Prepare macaroni according to package directions. Drain and return to saucepan. Add 1 cup cheese, evaporated milk, and seasonings; blend. Pour mixture into 2-quart baking dish, and sprinkle remaining ½ cup cheese on top. Bake 30 minutes or until hot and bubbly.

EASY CHEESE SAUCE
1 cup

1 cup (4 ounces) shredded
    process American
    cheese
¾ cup PET Evaporated Milk

In heavy saucepan, combine cheese and evaporated milk. Stir mixture over low heat until cheese is completely melted. Serve hot on baked potatoes, hot dogs, or other sandwiches.

152

HOT FUDGE SAUCE

1²/₃ cups   *(photograph on page 77)*

1 cup (6 ounces)
    WHITMAN'S Semi-Sweet
    Chocolate Chips
³/₄ cup PET Evaporated Milk
¹/₄ cup sugar
¹/₄ cup butter or margarine

In heavy saucepan, combine all ingredients. Stir over low heat until chocolate is completely melted. Serve warm.

SPICE AND RAISIN SAUCE

2 cups

1 cup water
¹/₂ cup raisins
¹/₂ cup sugar
¹/₈ teaspoon salt
2 tablespoons butter or
    margarine
1 tablespoon cornstarch
1 small can (5.33 fluid
    ounces) PET Evaporated
    Milk
¹/₂ teaspoon ground nutmeg

In small saucepan, combine water, raisins, sugar, and salt. Bring to a boil and remove from heat. In skillet, melt butter. Stir in cornstarch to form a smooth paste. Stir in evaporated milk and heat to a boil. Continue to cook 1 additional minute. Pour evaporated milk mixture into sugar mixture and blend well. Return to heat and cook over low heat 10 to 15 minutes or until mixture thickens. Mix in nutmeg. Serve sauce over B & M Boston Brown Bread or chilled fruit.

BUTTERSCOTCH SAUCE

2 cups

1¹/₄ cups firmly packed
    brown sugar
²/₃ cup white corn syrup
¹/₄ cup butter
³/₄ cup PET Evaporated Milk

In medium saucepan, combine brown sugar, corn syrup, and butter. Over medium heat, bring mixture to a boil and cook until it reaches thread stage (230°F). Remove from heat and cool 5 minutes. Beat in evaporated milk, mixing thoroughly. Serve sauce over vanilla ice cream.

CHOCOLATE MARSHMALLOW SAUCE

1 ½ cups

**2 cups miniature
    marshmallows
1 cup (6 ounces)
    WHITMAN'S Semi-Sweet
    Chocolate Chips
¼ cup sugar
1 small can (5.33 fluid
    ounces) PET Evaporated
    Milk
2 tablespoons butter
1 teaspoon vanilla
    Dash salt**

In heavy saucepan or double boiler, combine all ingredients. Cook over medium heat, stirring constantly until marshmallows have melted. Continue to cook until thickened. Serve warm over ice cream.

NOTE: *Twenty large marshmallows may be used in place of the miniature marshmallows.*

Americans are eating out more, and quite often it's Pet Food Service that brings them the foods they enjoy away from home. On-the-go lifestyles have brought about a great change in eating habits in recent years.

Pet's products are on the menu in many popular restaurants and school cafeterias. But that's just the beginning. You can find us almost everywhere. On airlines and in hospitals, nursing homes, theme restaurants, or convenience stores, you may be sampling something good from Pet without even knowing it. There's one place you *will* see our name, and that's at football or baseball stadiums across the country as you enjoy a growing favorite — our nachos served in distinctive red-and-yellow OLD EL PASO trays.

Whether it's Mexican food, frozen waffles, baked beans, or one of our other popular lines, America's demand for tasty, trusted food products in many places outside the home is growing.

APPLE TORTE

2 tortes, ½ torte per serving

1 package (3 ounces)
 cream cheese, softened
2 tablespoons sugar
8 DOWNYFLAKE Toaster
 Pancakes
1 cup apple pie filling
 Shredded toasted coconut
 Chopped nuts

In small bowl, combine cream cheese and sugar until well blended. Divide mixture into quarters. Prepare pancakes according to package directions. Spread 1 pancake with ¼ cup pie filling. Top pie filling with another pancake. Spread with one-quarter of the cream cheese mixture. Sprinkle generously with toasted coconut and chopped nuts. Top with another pancake, and spread with ¼ cup pie filling. Top with another pancake and spread with another quarter of the cream cheese mixture. Garnish with coconut and nuts. Repeat layers with remaining ingredients to make another torte. Serve immediately.

PINEAPPLE PARFAIT PIE

8 servings

1 can (8¼ ounces)
 crushed pineapple,
 divided usage
1 package (3 ounces)
 lemon gelatin
1 pint PET Vanilla
 Ice Cream
1 PET-RITZ Graham
 Pie Crust Shell
 PET WHIP Non-Dairy
 Whipped Topping,
 thawed

Drain pineapple, reserving liquid. Add enough water to liquid to measure 1 cup. In saucepan over medium heat, bring liquid to a boil. Remove from heat. Add gelatin; stir until gelatin is dissolved. Add vanilla ice cream by spoonfuls, stirring after each addition until melted. Chill until mixture mounds when spooned. Fold in crushed pineapple. Turn into graham crust. Chill 2½ to 3 hours or until set. Just before serving, garnish with PET WHIP.

Apple Torte

PUMPKIN PIE
6 servings   *(photograph on page 141)*

**1 cup firmly packed
    brown sugar
2 tablespoons all-purpose
    flour
2 1/4 teaspoons pumpkin
    pie spice
1/2 teaspoon salt
1 egg
1 can (16 ounces) solid-
    pack pumpkin
1 tall can (12 fluid ounces)
    PET Evaporated Milk
1 PET-RITZ Deep Dish
    Pie Crust Shell
    PET WHIP Non-Dairy
    Whipped Topping,
    thawed (optional)**

Preheat oven and cookie sheet to 375°F. In large bowl, mix brown sugar, flour, pumpkin pie spice, and salt. Stir in egg. Beat in pumpkin and evaporated milk until smooth. Pour into pie crust. Bake on preheated cookie sheet 50 to 55 minutes or until knife inserted one inch from edge comes out clean. Serve warm or cold, topped with PET WHIP if desired.

NOTE: *In place of pumpkin pie spice, you may use 1¼ teaspoons ground cinnamon, ½ teaspoon ground nutmeg, ½ teaspoon ground ginger, and ¼ teaspoon ground cloves.*

Pumpkins, Pumpkins Everywhere
We may never know who invented pumpkin pie, but many believe we have the Pilgrims to thank. Captain John Smith learned from the Indians how to grow pumpkins, and by 1683 they were such a staple that one poetic colonist rhymed, "We had pumpkins in the morning and pumpkins at noon. If it were not for pumpkins, we'd be undone soon." Now almost every Thanksgiving feast includes a satiny-smooth pumpkin pie in tribute to the Pilgrims' first Thanksgiving.

"HEARTY" CHOCOLATE CHIP COOKIES
Approximately 5 dozen cookies

1 1/2 cups all-purpose flour
1 teaspoon salt
1/2 teaspoon baking soda
1 cup butter or margarine,
     softened
3/4 cup firmly packed
     brown sugar
1/2 cup granulated sugar
2 eggs
1 teaspoon vanilla
2 cups HEARTLAND Natural
     Cereal, any variety
1 package (12 ounces)
     WHITMAN'S Semi-Sweet
     Chocolate Chips
1 cup chopped nuts

In small bowl, stir together flour, salt, and baking soda. In large mixing bowl, cream together butter or margarine, and sugars. Add eggs and vanilla, and beat until smooth. Mix in flour mixture, and blend well. Stir in HEARTLAND cereal, chocolate chips, and nuts. Refrigerate batter about 1 hour or until chilled. Drop chilled batter by teaspoonfuls onto greased cookie sheets. Bake at 375°F 10 minutes. Remove to cooling racks. Cool completely before storing.

CARAMEL BREAD PUDDING
6 to 8 servings

2 tablespoons butter or
     margarine
1 1/2 cups firmly packed
     brown sugar,
     divided usage
6 slices white bread,
     cut in 1/2-inch cubes
6 eggs
1 tall can (12 fluid ounces)
     PET Evaporated Milk
1/3 cup water
1 teaspoon vanilla
1/8 teaspoon salt

Preheat oven to 325°F. Generously butter shallow 1 1/2-quart casserole. Dot bottom with remaining butter. Sprinkle 1 cup brown sugar over bottom. Top with bread cubes. Beat eggs with wire whisk. Stir in remaining 1/2 cup brown sugar, evaporated milk, water, vanilla, and salt. Pour over bread cubes. Do not stir. Place casserole in larger pan. Pour hot water into pan one inch deep. Bake 45 to 50 minutes or until knife inserted one inch from edge comes out clean. Serve warm or cold.

SEGO LITE FROST
1 serving

1 can (10 fluid ounces) SEGO LITE Vanilla, chilled
1 scoop sherbert
1 cup ice

In blender container, combine all ingredients. Cover and process on HIGH until smooth and frothy.

MINT CHIP ICE CREAM
2 quarts

3 eggs
1 1/2 cups sugar
2 tall cans (12 fluid ounces) each) PET Evaporated Milk
3/4 teaspoon peppermint extract
1/8 teaspoon green food coloring
1 1/2 cups grated milk chocolate

In large mixing bowl, beat together eggs and sugar until well blended. Stir in evaporated milk, peppermint extract, and food coloring. Gently stir in grated chocolate. Refrigerate until well chilled. Pour into ice cream freezer container. Churn and freeze according to manufacturer's directions.

SEGO

Diet food offered little encouragement to Americans living in the early sixties. The only available reduced-calorie foods were sold through drugstores in limited flavors. Consumers soon became bored with the lack of variety and the persistent problem of hunger pangs. Then in 1961, Pet introduced the now popular line of SEGO liquid diet foods and sold them as a "fashion" food through grocery stores. SEGO, available in a delicious array of flavors, provided the variety needed to combat boredom, plus extra bulk to ward off hunger. For the first time, good taste, satisfaction, and reduced calories could all be found in the same can. And consumers were offered the promise of not only feeling better, but looking better, too.

SEGO LITE Frost

VANILLA ICE CREAM
2 quarts

2 eggs
¾ cup sugar
**2 tall cans (12 fluid
    ounces each) PET
    Evaporated Milk**
1 cup whole milk
1 tablespoon vanilla

In large mixing bowl, beat together eggs and sugar until well blended. Stir in evaporated milk, whole milk, and vanilla. Refrigerate until well chilled. Pour into ice cream freezer container. Churn and freeze according to manufacturer's directions. Serve plain or topped with Chocolate Marshmallow Sauce (page 153), Butterscotch Sauce (page 152), or Hot Fudge Sauce (page 152).

TO MAKE WITHOUT AN ICE CREAM FREEZER:
3 cups

1 egg
½ cup sugar
**1 tall can (12 fluid ounces)
    PET Evaporated Milk**
1 tablespoon lemon juice
1 tablespoon vanilla

Beat together egg and sugar until thick and light yellow in color. Stir in evaporated milk. Freeze until ice crystals form along edge. Beat in lemon juice and vanilla. Continue to beat until mixture doubles in bulk. Pour into 8-inch square dish. Freeze. Stir every 20 minutes to allow ice crystals to form uniformly. Freeze until firm.

Immortal Mascot
The tin cow has been associated with PET Evaporated Milk even longer than the name PET. A cow's head appeared on an early label of a milk that went under the name of "Tin Cow Brand." When "Our PET Brand" was adopted in 1894, the cow's head was pictured poking out from a toppled can. From that day to this, our label has changed many times, but our friendly cow's head still emerges from a pictured can.

CINNAMON CHOCOLATE ICE CREAM
2 quarts

3 tall cans (12 fluid ounces each) PET Evaporated Milk, divided usage
2 1/2 squares (1 ounce each) WHITMAN'S Unsweetened Baking Chocolate
2 eggs
1 cup sugar
1/2 teaspoon ground cinnamon
1/4 teaspoon ground nutmeg

In small saucepan, combine 1 can evaporated milk and chocolate. Cook over medium heat, stirring frequently, until chocolate melts and mixture is smooth. Meanwhile, beat eggs, sugar, cinnamon, and nutmeg in large mixing bowl until well blended. Stir in hot chocolate mixture. Stir in remaining 2 cans evaporated milk. Refrigerate until well chilled. Pour into ice cream freezer container. Churn and freeze according to manufacturer's directions.

CREAMY PRALINE ICE CREAM
2 quarts

4 eggs
2 1/2 cups sugar, divided usage
4 tall cans (12 fluid ounces each) PET Evaporated Milk, divided usage
3 tablespoons vanilla, divided usage
1/4 cup butter or margarine
1 tablespoon all-purpose flour
1 cup chopped pecans

Beat eggs and stir in 1 1/2 cups sugar. In saucepan, heat 5 cups evaporated milk until bubbles appear along edge. Gradually beat about 2 cups of hot evaporated milk into egg mixture. Return mixture to saucepan. Cook and stir over low heat until mixture thickens slightly. Remove from heat. Refrigerate until well chilled. Stir in 2 tablespoons vanilla. Pour into ice cream freezer container. Churn and freeze according to manufacturer's directions. Meanwhile, melt butter in 10-inch skillet. Stir in remaining 1 cup sugar. Add flour and cook over medium heat, stirring constantly. When mixture is light caramel in color and butter begins separating, stir in remaining 1 cup evaporated milk in a steady stream while mixture is boiling. Boil and stir until smooth and caramel colored. Remove from heat. Stir in remaining 1 tablespoon vanilla. Cool to room temperature. When ice cream is finished, swirl in caramel sauce and pecans.

CREAMY VANILLA FROSTING

1¾ cups frosting, enough for one 9-inch layer cake

**¹/₂ cup butter or margarine,
    softened**
¹/₄ cup PET Evaporated Milk
2 teaspoons vanilla
**4 cups (1 pound)
    confectioners sugar**

In 1½-quart mixing bowl, combine butter, evaporated milk, and vanilla. Add confectioners sugar, 1 cup at a time, mixing until smooth after each addition. Mix until frosting is smooth and shiny. If consistency is too thick, add a few drops of evaporated milk.

VARIATIONS: *Use one of the following in place of vanilla:*

Lemon: 1 tablespoon lemon juice and 1⅓ teaspoons grated lemon peel.

Orange: 1 tablespoon orange juice and 1½ teaspoons grated orange peel.

Peanut Butter: ⅓ cup chunky-style peanut butter and ⅓ cup (instead of ¼ cup) PET Evaporated Milk.

Chocolate: ⅓ cup unsweetened cocoa powder or two 1-ounce squares WHITMAN'S Unsweetened Baking Chocolate, melted, and ⅓ cup (instead of ¼ cup) PET Evaporated Milk.

Mocha: 2 teaspoons instant coffee granules.

Almond: ½ teaspoon almond extract.

Tutti-Frutti: ¼ cup cut-up mixed candied fruit and ⅓ cup (instead of ¼ cup) PET Evaporated Milk.

Cherry: 2 tablespoons finely chopped maraschino cherries, well drained.

Maple: ¼ teaspoon maple flavoring.

Nutmeg: 1 teaspoon ground nutmeg.

FAMOUS CREAMY MARSHMALLOW FUDGE

64 squares   *(photograph on page 141)*

2 cups sugar
1 small can (5.33 fluid ounces) PET Evaporated Milk
16 large marshmallows
¹/₄ teaspoon salt
1 cup (6 ounces) WHITMAN'S Semi-Sweet Chocolate Chips
¹/₂ cup chopped nuts (optional)
¹/₄ cup butter
1 teaspoon vanilla

Butter bottom and sides of 9-inch square pan. In heavy saucepan, combine sugar, evaporated milk, marshmallows, and salt. Heat mixture over medium heat until boiling, stirring constantly. When bubbles cover entire surface, continue to boil 5 additional minutes, stirring constantly. Remove from heat, and beat in chocolate chips, nuts if desired, butter, and vanilla. Continue to beat until chocolate is completely melted. Spread mixture into buttered pan. Chill until firm. Keep refrigerated until ready to serve.

FUDGE MARLOW ICE CREAM

2 quarts

1 tall can (12 fluid ounces) PET Evaporated Milk, divided usage
²/₃ cup sugar
¹/₃ cup unsweetened cocoa powder
Few grains salt
¹/₂ cup water
16 large marshmallows
2 teaspoons vanilla

In small mixing bowl, freeze 1 cup evaporated milk until ice crystals form along edge. In small saucepan, stir together sugar, cocoa, and salt. Add remaining evaporated milk and water. Cook and stir over low heat until smooth. Add marshmallows and cook until half melted. Remove from heat. Stir until completely melted. Stir in vanilla. Pour into medium bowl. Refrigerate until well chilled. Beat icy evaporated milk until stiff. Fold into chilled cocoa mixture. Pour into 2½-quart bowl. Freeze until firm.

FUDGE SUNDAE PIE

8 to 10 servings

1 cup PET Evaporated Milk
1 cup (6 ounces)
    WHITMAN'S Semi-Sweet
    Chocolate Chips
¼ teaspoon salt
1 cup miniature
    marshmallows
30 vanilla wafers
4 cups PET Vanilla Ice
    Cream, softened
Almond halves

In heavy saucepan, combine evaporated milk, chocolate chips, and salt. Stir over low heat until chocolate melts completely and mixture thickens. Remove from heat and add marshmallows. Stir rapidly until marshmallows melt and mixture is smooth. Cool to room temperature. Line the bottom and sides of 9-inch pie pan with vanilla wafers. Spread half the ice cream over wafers. Cover with half the chocolate mixture. Repeat with remaining ice cream and chocolate. Garnish with almonds. Freeze at least 5 hours or until firm.

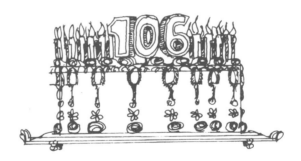

Centenarian

One woman's life has spanned the entire century of Pet's existence. Jennie Latzer Kaeser, daughter of a Pet founder and early president Louis Latzer, is 106 years old as this book goes to press. Mrs. Kaeser resides in her country home near Highland, Illinois, and like her father, has been an important benefactor to the city of Highland. Her contributions have included adding a wing and a children's room to the library that the Latzer family presented to Highland in Louis Latzer's memory.

Brandied Beans (page 176), Cheese and Vegetable Spaghetti (page 166), Elegant Tuna Quiche (page 181), Orange Stir-and-Bake Cake (page 185)

Say, Have You Got a Minute?

166

Say, Have You Got a Minute? Say, Have You Got a Minute? Say, Have You Got a Minute

SPAGHETTI MARINE

6 servings

8 ounces spaghetti, broken
2 cans (4¼ ounces each)
ORLEANS Deveined
Medium or Large
Shrimp, drained
2 tablespoons butter or
margarine
2 tablespoons all-purpose
flour
½ teaspoon dillweed
½ teaspoon salt
1 tall can (12 fluid ounces)
PET Evaporated Milk
½ cup water
1 tablespoon white wine
1 tablespoon minced parsley
Grated Parmesan cheese

Cook spaghetti according to package directions. Drain and rinse with cold water. Rinse shrimp in cold running water. Drain. In medium saucepan, melt butter. Blend in flour, dillweed, and salt. Slowly add evaporated milk and water. Bring to a boil. Boil 1 minute, stirring frequently. Add spaghetti and shrimp. Heat thoroughly. Remove from heat. Stir in wine and parsley. Sprinkle with cheese. Serve immediately.

CHEESE AND VEGETABLE SPAGHETTI

4 servings   *(photograph on page 165)*

1 package (10 ounces)
spaghetti
2 cans (13.3 ounces each)
COMPLIMENT White
Sauce
1 package (10 ounces) frozen
peas, thawed
1½ cups (6 ounces) cubed
cooked ham
1 cup (4 ounces) shredded
Fontina cheese
1 cup (4 ounces) shredded
Mozzarella cheese
1 teaspoon thyme
½ teaspoon oregano
Freshly ground black
pepper to taste

Prepare spaghetti according to package directions. Drain and keep warm. In saucepan over low heat, mix COMPLIMENT, peas, ham, cheeses, thyme, oregano, and pepper, stirring until cheese melts. In large bowl, toss spaghetti and cheese sauce until spaghetti is well coated. Serve immediately.

EASY FETTUCCINE

4 servings

6 ounces medium or fine egg noodles
2 tablespoons butter or margarine
Salt and freshly ground black pepper to taste
1 can (13.3 fluid ounces) COMPLIMENT White Sauce
1 cup (4 ounces) shredded Swiss cheese
Grated Parmesan cheese
Parsley sprigs (optional)

Cook noodles according to package directions. Drain. Return noodles to pan and add butter, salt, and pepper. Toss to blend. In separate saucepan, stir together COMPLIMENT and Swiss cheese. Heat until cheese is melted. Pour sauce mixture over noodles and toss again. To serve, sprinkle with grated Parmesan cheese. Garnish with parsley sprigs if desired.

EASY LASAGNA CASSEROLE

8 to 10 servings

4 cups large egg noodles
1 pound lean ground beef
1/2 cup chopped onions
1 can (15 ounces) tomato sauce
1 package (1 1/2 ounces) spaghetti sauce mix
1 cup PET Evaporated Milk
1 package (3 ounces) cream cheese, softened
1/2 teaspoon garlic salt
1 cup (4 ounces) shredded Mozzarella cheese

Prepare noodles according to package directions; drain. In large skillet, brown ground beef and onions. Drain off fat. Stir in tomato sauce and spaghetti sauce mix, and cook mixture over medium heat until it begins to thicken. In saucepan, heat evaporated milk and cream cheese until smooth. Remove from heat and stir in cooked noodles and garlic salt. Pour noodle mixture into 11 × 7-inch baking dish. Spread meat mixture over noodles. Top with shredded cheese. Bake at 350°F 20 minutes or until bubbly.

MICROWAVE DIRECTIONS: *Microwave on HIGH 8 to 10 minutes or until steaming. Turn 3 to 4 times during cooking time.*

168

Say, Have You Got a Minute? Say, Have You Got a Minute? Say, Have You Got a Minut

PIZZA TREATS
8 pizza treats

1 can (8 ounces) tomato
    sauce
1 can (4³/₄ ounces)
    UNDERWOOD Roast
    Beef Spread
2 tablespoons grated onion
¹/₂ teaspoon oregano
    Dash garlic powder
4 English muffins, split and
    toasted
1 cup (4 ounces) shredded
    Monterey Jack or
    Mozzarella cheese

In small bowl, mix tomato sauce, roast beef spread, onion, oregano, and garlic powder. Spread tomato mixture on toasted muffins and top with cheese. Place muffins on baking sheet and broil about 4 inches from heat until hot and bubbly.

SARDINE ITALIANO
8 snacks

3 cans (3³/₄ ounces each)
    UNDERWOOD Sardines,
    in Tomato Sauce or in
    Soya Bean Oil, drained
4 hamburger buns
    Butter or margarine,
    softened
¹/₂ cup catsup
1 tablespoon diced onion
¹/₂ teaspoon oregano
    Dash garlic powder
    (optional)
1 cup (4 ounces) shredded
    Mozzarella cheese

Preheat oven to 450°F. Cut sardines into bite-size pieces. Split buns and spread each half with softened butter. Place buns, buttered side up, on baking sheet. Arrange sardines on top. Combine catsup, onion, oregano, and garlic powder if desired. Spoon about one tablespoon seasoned catsup over sardines on each bun half. Top with cheese. Bake 8 to 10 minutes or until cheese melts and buns are toasted. Serve hot.

Short-Cut
The word "can" may have been coined by a weary secretary for the Wm. Underwood Company. The story goes that the secretary grew tired of entering the full word "canister" in company ledgers, and began writing "can" instead. The abbreviation caught on, and the word became a part of our everyday vocabulary.

HAVE A FIESTA!

Even when you're in a hurry, you can still enjoy quality Mexican food. For your convenience, OLD EL PASO has developed a line of frozen Mexican entrees which are available in the freezer section of your grocery store. These tasty products can be worked into an American menu or blended into a complete Mexican fiesta dinner.

The following menus will help you get started in using time-saving, delicious, frozen products from OLD EL PASO.

Cheesy Tomato Soup (page 179)
OLD EL PASO Frozen Beef and Bean Burrito
Tossed Green Salad
OLD EL PASO NACHIPS Tortilla Chips
Iced Tea
Fudge Brownies (page 18)

OLD EL PASO Frozen Enchiladas (any variety)
Mixed Vegetables
Sour Cream Bran Muffins (page 75)
Water or Dinner Wine
Luscious Peach Pie (page 184)

OLD EL PASO Frozen Enchiladas (any variety)
OLD EL PASO Refried Beans topped with Shredded Cheese
Gazpacho Salad (page 144)
OLD EL PASO NACHIPS Tortilla Chips
Sangria
Cinnamon Chocolate Ice Cream (page 161)

OLD EL PASO Frozen Chimichangas (any variety)
topped with your choice of:
Shredded Cheddar Cheese   OLD EL PASO Picante Salsa
Hot Sour Cream   Guacamole (page 201)
Fresh Fruit Cup
Mexican Corn Bread (page 134)
Lemonade
Coffee Liqueur Pie (page 214)

ou Got a Minute? Say, Have You Got a

171

TACO SCRAMBLER

2 servings

4 OLD EL PASO Taco Shells
¼ cup chopped green onions
2 tablespoons butter or
    margarine
4 eggs, beaten
¼ cup milk
¼ cup chopped tomato
3 tablespoons OLD EL PASO
    Chopped Green Chilies
½ teaspoon salt
1 jar (8 ounces) pasteurized
    process cheese spread,
    heated
  OLD EL PASO Taco Sauce

Crisp taco shells by baking at 350°F 5 to 7 minutes. In skillet, sauté green onions in butter until tender. Beat together eggs, milk, tomato, green chilies, and salt. Add egg mixture to sautéed green onion. Cook, stirring occasionally, until eggs are firm. Spoon egg mixture into taco shells and top with cheese spread and taco sauce.

Chili Raid

"Do you have any green chili?" asked the FBI agents, flashing identity cards. The time was early 1945 and the place was the Mountain Pass Canning Company (forerunner of our own OLD EL PASO brand) in Canutillo, Texas. There was a wartime restriction on the use of tin cans, and that restriction included the canning of green chilies.

"I could practically see myself behind bars," recalled one of the owners. He admitted to canning some chilies experimentally, and the agents responded, "Great! Can we buy a couple of cases? We haven't had any since before the war." They got their chilies and all was well.

Taco Scrambler

A sprightly Red Devil dances on the label, and inside the elegantly wrapped can, UNDERWOOD Deviled Ham — or chicken, roast beef, liverwurst, or corned beef spreads — are ready for smoothing on bread or crackers for quick, tasty sandwiches, hors d'oeuvres, or canapes.

Our Red Devil has seen quite a few changes over the years. America's oldest registered food trademark still in use today first came to life in 1867 as a stocky, leering demon with cloven hoof. In various metamorphoses, he has slimmed down, donned slippers, picked up a pitchfork, and lost his scowl. Through it all, he has presided over a company that itself has seen phenomenal change and growth since the auspicious day in March 1822 when William Underwood set up shop on Boston's Russia Wharf.

When Underwood began pickling and preserving fruits, condiments, sauces, and other delicacies, his first challenge was to win the heart of the American housewife. His process of preparing fine products with slow, careful attention to taste and health seemed to ask the housewife to let

someone else lend a hand in the kitchen — a novel idea in those days. But the Underwood products not only tasted good, they also contributed important vitamins and minerals to the American diet, which was long on meat, cheese, and alcohol, short on milk, fruit, and fresh vegetables. Soon, nutritive value and superior quality had made a name for the UNDERWOOD brand.

By the mid-1800s, the young company was canning and preserving all manner of seafood, meat, fruits, and vegetables. UNDERWOOD preserves were being traded in the West Indies, South America, the Far East, and the countries of the Mediterranean. At home, they were among the staples carried on the nation's westward march. Tins of canned meat and fruit traveled by clipper ship to the Forty-Niners seeking gold in California. In fact, legend has it that the first gold nugget smuggled east was concealed in an empty UNDERWOOD salmon can.

After the pioneers and prospectors came America's explorers and adventurers, and on virtually every major expedition — whether to mountain peak or frozen pole, Underwood's lightweight, nutritious products were sure to be found among the essential provisions.

With the advent of the Civil War, Underwood had lost its large Southern market. In an attempt to attract new customers, it introduced its famous line of highly seasoned meat products, made with a special mixture of spices known as "deviling." The recipe for deviling was a closely guarded

"family secret" — and remains one even today. That secret recipe opened the way for a startling new lunchtime food — the sandwich.

Before the introduction of that novel idea, the tin canister, or "can," had encountered even greater skepticism. Early 19th century Americans were used to glass containers and were afraid food would spoil in cans. But William Underwood refused to use quick canning methods and instead insisted on a slow, safer process. Decades later, his grandson William Lyman teamed up with biologist Samuel Prescott of the Massachusetts Institute of Technology. Together they perfected the food sterilization process that would influence the entire food processing industry. In fact, their experiments and improvements are credited with turning food processing from an art into a science.

As Underwood grew and prospered, it moved to larger quarters in Watertown, Massachusetts. Many other old and established firms came under the Underwood wing, including Richardson and Robbins, makers of high-quality canned chicken products; Burham & Morrill, of B&M Baked

That Wonderful
Sandwich of
UNDERWOOD Pure Deviled Ham

Beans fame; Ac'cent International; and C. Shippam Limited of England. Other overseas trademarks were acquired, including, in France, Chevallier-Appert, the world's first and oldest canner. Food processing expanded to Canada, Mexico, Australia, Norway, and Venezuela. The products of Underwood's Venezuela company, DIABLITOS, are today enjoyed by over 90 percent of Venezuelans.

In 1982, Underwood joined the Pet family of products. Its well-established reputation for producing only the highest quality products — products that for over 150 years have been saving the American cook time and toil — made it a perfect addition to our family. And its popularity all around the world brings us new friends and customers in many lands.

Today, Underwood concentrates on producing seven popular items: Deviled Ham, Chunky Chicken Spread, Corned Beef Spread, Liverwurst Spread, Roast Beef Spread, and three varieties of canned sardines. In fact, as we celebrate Pet's 100th anniversary, we're also proud to salute over a century of canning sardines under the UNDERWOOD label.

Whether it's canned sardines, Deviled Ham, or Chunky Chicken Spread, when you serve an UNDERWOOD product, you may be sure you'll receive many smiles of appreciation — including one from our own Red Devil.

174

Say, Have You Got a Minute? Say, Have You Got a Minute? Say, Have You Got a Minute

REUBEN UNDERWOOD
4 open-faced sandwiches

**2 cans (4 1/2 ounces each)
UNDERWOOD Corned
Beef Spread
4 teaspoons prepared
mustard
4 slices rye bread
1 can (8 ounces) sauerkraut,
well drained
4 slices Swiss cheese**

In small bowl, mix corned beef spread and mustard. Spread on 4 slices of bread. Top each slice with sauerkraut and 1 slice of cheese. Broil 5 inches from heat until cheese is melted and bubbly.

PROSPERITY SANDWICH
6 servings

**2 1/4 cups (9 ounces) diced
process American
cheese
1 cup PET Evaporated Milk
1 teaspoon dry mustard
1 teaspoon Worcestershire
sauce
6 slices toast
6 slices turkey
12 slices bacon, fried crisp
and drained**

To prepare cheese sauce, combine cheese, evaporated milk, mustard, and Worcestershire sauce in 2-quart saucepan. Stir over medium heat until cheese melts. Place 1 slice of toast on each individual plate. Cover toast with 1 slice of turkey, then pour cheese sauce over. Top with bacon slices.

NOTE: *Other cheeses may be used. Top with cooked asparagus, if desired.*

BARBECUE BEEF BUNS
6 sandwiches

**1 can (4 3/4 ounces)
UNDERWOOD Roast
Beef Spread
1/4 cup chopped celery
1/4 cup barbecue sauce
2 tablespoons chopped onion
6 club rolls (4 inches round),
split and toasted**

In saucepan, mix roast beef spread, celery, barbecue sauce, and onion. Cook over medium heat until steaming. Serve on toasted rolls.

Reuben UNDERWOOD, Duchess Potato Salad (page 98)

176

BEANS AND HAM ALOHA
6 servings

**1 can (28 ounces) B&M Brick
   Oven Baked Beans**
**1 fully cooked ham steak
   (1 1/2 pounds), cut into
   bite-size pieces**
2 pineapple rings, halved
2 tablespoons brown sugar

Preheat oven to 350°F. In large bowl, combine beans and ham. Pour into 2-quart casserole. Top with pineapple and sprinkle with brown sugar. Bake 30 minutes.

MICROWAVE DIRECTIONS: *Combine ingredients as directed above in microwave safe casserole. Microwave on HIGH 10 to 12 minutes or until steaming. Turn casserole 4 times during cooking time to ensure even heating.*

BRANDIED BEANS
6 servings

(photograph on page 165)

**1 can (28 ounces) B&M Brick
   Oven Baked Beans**
1 can (1 pound) peach halves
**1/4 cup brandy
   Whole cloves**

Preheat oven to 350°F. Place beans in 2-quart casserole and top with peach halves. Pour brandy over peaches and stud with cloves. Bake 30 minutes.

BEAN BURGERS
6 bean burgers

1 pound lean ground beef
**1/4 cup chopped green
   pepper**
1/4 cup chopped onion
**1 can (28 ounces) B&M Brick
   Oven Baked Beans**
**6 hamburger rolls, split
   and toasted**

In medium skillet, brown ground beef with green pepper and onion. Drain. Add beans to meat mixture and heat until warm. Serve mixture sandwiched between halves of toasted rolls.

177

/ou Got a Minute? Say, Have You Got a

SKILLET SCALLOPED POTATOES
Four 1-cup servings

3 tablespoons vegetable oil
4 cups diced frozen
    hashed brown potatoes
¹/₄ cup chopped onion
1 ¹/₂ teaspoons salt
    Dash black pepper
1 cup PET Evaporated Milk
2 tablespoons snipped parsley

In skillet, heat oil over medium heat. Add potatoes, onion, salt, and pepper. Brown potatoes. Add evaporated milk and parsley. Lower heat, and cook slowly 5 additional minutes or until sauce thickens. Serve hot.

For our forefathers in New England, sundown Saturday to sundown Sunday was a time of rest and worship. Beans could be cooked all day Saturday and kept warm in the fireplace for Sunday's meal. In time, the Pilgrims found they could add flavor to this traditional meal by taking their bean pots to the corner baker, who would slow-bake the beans in his brick oven. Centuries later, in Portland, Maine, a small company was founded that would become America's number one maker of brick-oven baked beans — Burham & Morrill Co., better known as B&M.

As a canner of meats, fish, and vegetables — especially corn — B&M earned a reputation for consistent quality. By the 1920s the corn center of the United States had shifted to the Midwest, and Northeast-based B&M switched from corn to its famous brick-oven baked beans, made with a patented seven-hour baking process.

Four decades later, another venerable New Englander — the Wm. Underwood Company — acquired B&M, and in 1982 Underwood and B&M brought their respected names and fine foods to the Pet family.

EASY SHRIMP CHOWDER

4 servings

1 can (4¹/₄ ounces) ORLEANS
   Deveined Medium
   Shrimp
¹/₄ cup thinly sliced celery
2 tablespoons chopped
   onion
1 tablespoon butter or
   margarine
1 tall can (12 fluid ounces)
   PET Evaporated Milk
1 can (10³/₄ ounces) cream of
   potato soup

Rinse shrimp under cold running water.
Drain. Sauté celery and onion in butter
until tender. Stir in evaporated milk, potato
soup, and shrimp. Heat, stirring often, until
hot, but do not boil.

MICROWAVE DIRECTIONS: *In 3-quart
microwave safe casserole, microwave celery and
onion in butter on HIGH 3 minutes or until
tender. Stir in evaporated milk, potato soup, and
shrimp. Mix well. Mircowave on HIGH 10 minutes
or until heated through. Stir 1 or 2 times during
cooking time. Let stand 5 minutes before serving.*

SPEEDY OYSTER STEW

4 servings

1 tall can (12 fluid ounces)
   PET Evaporated Milk
1 can (8 ounces) ORLEANS
   Louisiana Oysters
5 tablespoons butter
2 cups whole milk
2 teaspoons parsley flakes
1 teaspoon paprika
¹/₂ teaspoon salt
¹/₂ teaspoon freshly ground
   black pepper

Put all ingredients in saucepan. Heat to
steaming, but do not boil. Serve
immediately.

CHEESY TOMATO SOUP

2 to 3 servings

1 can (10³/₄ ounces) tomato
   soup
³/₄ cup PET Evaporated Milk
³/₄ cup pasteurized process
   cheese spread
¹/₂ cup water

In saucepan, combine all ingredients.
Stirring constantly, warm mixture over low
heat, but do not boil. Serve hot.

Easy Shrimp Chowder

SHRIMP AND OYSTER SUPREME
6 servings

1 can (4 1/4 ounces) ORLEANS
    Deveined Medium
    Shrimp
3/4 cup chopped green
    pepper
3/4 cup chopped onions
3/4 cup chopped celery
1/4 cup butter or margarine
1/4 cup all-purpose flour
1/2 teaspoon dry mustard
1/4 teaspoon salt
  Dash red pepper
1 tall can (12 fluid ounces)
    PET Evaporated Milk
1/2 cup water
1 can (8 ounces) ORLEANS
    Smoked Oysters, drained
1 tablespoon lemon juice
1 teaspoon Worcestershire
    sauce
3 cups warm cooked rice

Rinse shrimp in cold running water. Drain. In large skillet, cook green pepper, onions, and celery in butter just until tender. Stir in flour, dry mustard, salt, and red pepper. Gradually stir in evaporated milk and water. Heat to boiling. Boil 1 minute. Stir in oysters, shrimp, lemon juice, and Worcestershire sauce. Heat until steaming, stirring gently to avoid breaking shrimp. Serve over warm rice.

BREADED FISH FILLETS
6 servings

1 1/2 pounds fish fillets (cod,
    haddock, sole, perch,
    turbot)
1 small can (5.33 fluid
    ounces) PET Evaporated
    Milk
1 teaspoon salt
1/8 teaspoon freshly ground
    black pepper
3/4 cup fine corn flake crumbs

Preheat oven to 400°F. Cut fish fillets into individual portions. Dip each piece of fish in mixture of evaporated milk, salt, and pepper. Roll each piece of fish in corn flake crumbs. Place on greased baking sheet. Bake 20 minutes or until brown. Serve hot.

CHEESE AND CRAB DELIGHT

6 servings

2 tablespoons butter or margarine
2 tablespoons chopped green pepper
³/₄ teaspoon dry mustard
¹/₄ teaspoon salt
¹/₈ teaspoon cayenne pepper
1 cup cooked or canned tomatoes, strained or chopped
1 cup (4 ounces) shredded Cheddar cheese
1 egg, well beaten
³/₄ cup PET Evaporated Milk
2 cans (6 ounces each) ORLEANS Lump Crab Meat, drained
3 cups warm cooked rice

In medium saucepan, melt butter. Add green pepper, dry mustard, salt, and cayenne pepper. Cook 5 minutes on low heat. Stir in tomatoes, cheese, and egg. Cook an additional 5 minutes, stirring constantly. Add evaporated milk and crab meat. Heat thoroughly, but do not boil. Serve over warm rice.

ELEGANT TUNA QUICHE

6 servings

(photograph on page 165)

¹/₂ cup milk
¹/₂ cup mayonnaise or salad dressing
3 tablespoons white wine
2 eggs
3 tablespoons all-purpose flour
¹/₄ teaspoon salt (optional)
1 cup (4 ounces) shredded Swiss cheese
1 can (6¹/₂ ounces) tuna, drained
3 tablespoons chopped green pepper
1 PET-RITZ Regular Pie Crust Shell
Grated Parmesan cheese

Preheat oven and cookie sheet to 375°F. In medium bowl, combine milk, mayonnaise, wine, eggs, flour, and salt. Mix well with wire whisk. Stir in Swiss cheese, tuna, and green onion. Pour into pie crust shell. Bake on preheated cookie sheet 30 to 35 minutes. Sprinkle with Parmesan cheese. Cool 10 minutes before serving.

182

Say, Have You Got a Minute? Say, Have You Got a Minute? Say, Have You Got a Minute

SUNDAE SUPREME
4 sundaes

**4 DOWNYFLAKE Waffles,
    any variety
PET Vanilla Ice Cream
Hot Fudge Sauce (page 152)
PET WHIP Non-Dairy
    Whipped Topping,
    thawed
¹/₂ cup chopped nuts
4 maraschino cherries**

Toast waffles. Top each waffle with ice cream, Hot Fudge Sauce, PET WHIP, chopped nuts, and 1 cherry.

EASY STRAWBERRY SHORTCAKE
6 individual shortcakes

**1 pint strawberries, washed,
    hulled, and halved
2 tablespoons sugar
6 DOWNYFLAKE Waffles,
    any variety
PET WHIP Non-Dairy
    Whipped Topping,
    thawed**

Combine strawberries and sugar. Refrigerate mixture until chilled. When strawberries are chilled, toast waffles. Top each waffle with strawberries and PET WHIP.

Sundae Supreme

184

LUSCIOUS PEACH PIE

6 to 8 servings

1 package (8 ounces) cream cheese, softened
1 cup confectioners sugar
1/2 teaspoon almond extract
1 1/2 cups PET WHIP Non-Dairy Whipped Topping, thawed
1 can (16 ounces) sliced peaches, drained
1 PET-RITZ Graham Pie Crust Shell

In large mixing bowl, combine cream cheese, confectioners sugar, and almond extract. Beat until smooth. Gently fold in PET WHIP and peaches. Pour into graham crust. Chill until firm.

LIME WHIP PIE

6 to 8 servings

1 can (14 ounces) sweetened condensed milk
1 can (6 ounces) frozen limeade, thawed
1 cup PET WHIP Non-Dairy Whipped Topping, thawed
1 PET-RITZ Graham Pie Crust Shell
2 tablespoons chopped maraschino cherries

In mixing bowl, gradually combine sweetened condensed milk and limeade. Mix thoroughly. Fold in PET WHIP until well blended. Pour filling into graham crust. Chill several hours until firm. To serve, garnish with chopped maraschino cherries.

ORANGE STIR-AND-BAKE CAKE

9 servings   *(photograph on page 165)*

1 cup all-purpose flour
1 cup HEARTLAND Cereal,
    Coconut
2/3 cup sugar
1/3 cup instant nonfat·dry milk
1 teaspoon baking soda
1/2 teaspoon salt
1 cup orange juice
1/3 cup vegetable oil
1 teaspoon orange extract

Preheat oven to 375°F. In mixing bowl, stir together flour, HEARTLAND cereal, sugar, dry milk, baking soda, and salt. Add orange juice, oil, and orange extract. Stir until well blended. Pour into greased 8-inch square baking pan. Bake 30 to 40 minutes or until toothpick inserted near center comes out clean. Serve from pan. Sprinkle with confectioners sugar if desired.

The snack cake from a vending machine, the individual fruit pie from your local supermarket, the sweet roll served on your next airline flight — you may be surprised to learn that these fresh-baked goods could have something in common besides the homemade taste you've always enjoyed. They may also share a common home — the Bakery Division of Pet.

Our most popular brand is AUNT FANNY'S, named for the baking company that began as a tiny piemaker in Atlanta, Georgia, nearly four decades ago. In 1966 Aunt Fanny's brought its well-established name and good products to Pet. Aunt Fanny's most popular product is a sweet cinnamon-and-nut treat called PECAN TWIRLS — one bite and you'll have to have another! Other Bakery Division products go by names like Rustic Mill and PET. Some of our goodies go under the names of Jane Parker, Hostess, Mrs. Wright's, or Dixie Darling. Or they may go by no name at all, appearing as sweet silent partners with your airline, school cafeteria, or restaurant meal.

What's in a name? Whether it's PECAN TWIRLS, Honey Buns, Bogies, pie snacks, cupcakes, pound cakes, or strudel, your favorite fresh-baked snack may very well be just another branch on the Pet family tree.

186

Say, Have You Got a Minute? Say, Have You Got a Minute? Say, Have You Got a Minute

EASY LEMON POUND CAKE

10 to 12 servings

1 box (16 ounces) pound cake mix
¹/₃ cup PET Evaporated Milk
¹/₃ cup lemon juice
2 eggs
2 teaspoons grated lemon peel

Preheat oven to 325°F. In large bowl, combine all ingredients until moistened. Beat with electric mixer on HIGH 3 minutes. Pour into greased and floured 9 × 5-inch loaf pan. Bake 55 to 60 minutes or until top springs back when lightly touched. Serve plain or topped with Lemon Glaze.

LEMON GLAZE

1 ¹/₂ cups confectioners sugar
2 tablespoons PET Evaporated Milk
1 tablespoon lemon juice

Combine all ingredients. Mix until well blended. Glaze cake.

Beef Chili Cheese Braid (page 208), Jalapeño Cheese Ball with OLD EL PASO Tortilla Chips (page 203), Chocolate Fondue and Assorted Dippers (page 186), Mushroom Quiche (page 209)

Let's Have a Party!

Everybody loves a party!

Whether it's a small dinner for four or a large open house, the key to enjoying your party is careful advance planning.

One good way to plan for a party is to make up a *Party Planner*—a list of basic information that will serve as a handy checklist later on.

PREPARING THE PARTY PLANNER

For your Party Planner, you'll need to consider several basic details.

Occasion. What kind of party are you planning? A birthday, a bridal shower, a holiday celebration? Theme, color scheme, and decoration ideas will start to flow once you focus your thoughts on the occasion.

Number of Guests. Will it be a formal, sit-down affair or a casual, family-style buffet? The amount of space you have available, plus your stock of dishes, glasses, flatware, and utensils will be important considerations when you make that decision.

Keep in mind the ages of your guests. Your planning will vary depending on whether your guests are all adults, teenagers, or children.

Whom Should You Invite?

The most successful parties seem to be those that bring together people who have something in common. They needn't all know one another — in fact, meeting new people can be half the fun.

Date and Time

The precise date and time are, of course, important to both you and your guests. You may be inviting your guests by phone, or for a more formal affair, by written invitation. If you are mailing invitations, be sure to plan enough time for addressing, mailing, and R.S.V.P.'s. And if your home is hard to find, directions or a map are sure to be appreciated.

Budget

Even for a small party, you must consider just how much you can afford to spend. Besides food and beverages, your expenses may include invitations, postage, flowers and decorations, extra help, and entertainment.

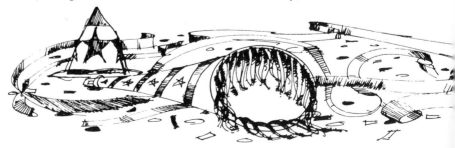

189

t's Have a Party! Let's Have a Party! Let's

Location

Parties held in halls, clubs, or other locations outside the home require reservations and other advance arrangements that must be on your time-table. You may be planning a summer supper on the patio, but give some thought to moving your party indoors if "Mother Nature" doesn't cooper-ate. Consider available serving space — perhaps you'll need to have boards cut to fit the top of a pool table or saw horses to create a serving table.

MENU PLANNING

To begin planning your party menu, you must first decide on the center of attention — the one special main dish or dessert that will add elegance and sparkle to your table.

Complement your "star" dish with foods selected for their contrasts in color, texture, size and shape, temperature, and taste.

Keep in mind these few important tips:
• Never experiment with a new recipe for a party.
• Make sure you have all the cooking utensils, serving dishes, and flatware you'll need for your planned menu.
• Never plan more than one dish that requires very close attention and careful timing.

Scheduling Your Time

A detailed time schedule will help you avoid last-minute, frenzied prep-arations. Start by writing your serving time at the bottom of a piece of paper, and then estimate cooking and preparation times for each recipe. Working backwards from the serving time, make a note of when you must begin preparation and cooking of each dish.

Remember these helpful hints:
• Take advantage of dishes that can be cooked ahead, like cakes or past-ries, or prepared ahead and held in the refrigerator or freezer, like salad greens or casseroles.
• Your table may be set the day before the party, with a sheet over the settings to keep everything bright and clean.

Preparing the Grocery List

You might find it helpful to organize your grocery list in the order of your supermarket's departments.

List all the ingredients needed for the preparation of each recipe; then add garnishes, like parsley, nuts, pickles, whipping cream, and cherries;

190

and finally accompaniments, like butter for bread and rolls, jams or chutneys, relishes, and candy.

And be kind to yourself — try not to leave shopping until the day of your party.

Setting the Table

Your table setting, whether elegant or simple, should reflect your tastes and preferences in an atmosphere that is natural and comfortable.

To help you set your party table, we've included some photographic guides.

- Page 211 shows you the traditional setting for a formal sit-down luncheon or dinner.
- Pages 193, 199, and 207 will give you some ideas for the setting of buffets for several occasions.

If convenience and common sense are your guides in setting the buffet table, your guests will be comfortable and well-served.

On Your Own

The pages that follow offer sample menus and table settings for a variety of occasions. Let our ideas guide you or use them simply to stimulate your own creative thinking. Remember, the key to a successful party is careful planning, and the host or hostess who is relaxed and prepared is the one most likely to set partygoers at ease. So plan ahead . . . and plan to enjoy yourself!

MEXI-PEANUTS

Approximately 1 quart   *(photograph on page 193)*

¹/₄ cup olive oil
1 package (1¹/₄ ounces)
    OLD EL PASO Taco
    Seasoning
1 garlic clove, minced
¹/₄ teaspoon cumin
6 drops hot pepper sauce
16 ounces salted blanched
    peanuts

In heavy skillet heat oil 1 minute. Add taco seasoning, garlic, cumin, and hot pepper sauce, stirring constantly. Add peanuts and stir over medium heat about 5 minutes. Store in covered container.

APPETIZER HOTS

36 appetizers

1 pound hot dogs
1 can (14 ounces) OLD EL
    PASO Enchilada Sauce
¹/₂ cup firmly packed brown
    sugar
1¹/₂ teaspoons cider vinegar
¹/₂ teaspoon Worcestershire
    sauce

Cut hot dogs into bite-size pieces about one inch in length. In saucepan, combine enchilada sauce, brown sugar, vinegar, and Worcestershire sauce. Add hot dogs to sauce, bring to a boil, and simmer, uncovered, 15 to 20 minutes. Pour into fondue pot, and keep warm. Serve with cocktail forks.

MICROWAVE DIRECTIONS: *Combine all ingredients in microwave safe bowl. Microwave on HIGH 7 to 8 minutes or until heated through, stirring every 2 minutes.*

MINI REUBENS

18 hors d'oeuvres   *(photograph on page 193)*

18 slices party rye bread
1 can (4¹/₄ ounces)
    UNDERWOOD Corned
    Beef Spread
2 teaspoons prepared
    mustard
¹/₂ teaspoon instant minced
    onion
18 slices Swiss cheese
    (2×2 inches)

In broiler, toast one side of rye slices. In small bowl, mix corned beef spread, mustard, and onion; spread on untoasted side of bread. Top with cheese slices, and broil 3 to 5 minutes or until cheese melts. Serve hot.

192

Let's Have a Party! Let's Have a Party! Let's Have a Party! Let's Have a Party! Let's Ha

Cocktail Party Menu:

Dilly Shrimp Cheese Ball (page 202)

OLD EL PASO NACHIPS Tortilla Chips

Beef and Bean Empañadas (page 196)

Appetizer Hots (page 191)

Mini Reubens (page 191)

Spicy Cheese Dip (page 200)

Assorted Raw Vegetables

Mexi-Peanuts (page 191)

WHITMAN'S Assorted Candy

Beverage Service

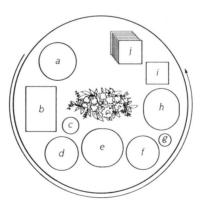

COCKTAIL PARTY

a) *Plates* b) *Mini Reubens* c) *Mexi-Peanuts*
d) *WHITMAN'S Assorted Candy*
e) *Spicy Cheese Dip and Assorted Vegetables*
f) *Appetizer Hots* g) *Cocktail Forks* h) *Dilly Shrimp Cheese
Ball and OLD EL PASO NACHIP Tortilla Chips*
i) *Beef and Bean Empañadas* j) *Napkins*

Spicy Cheese Dip with Assorted Vegetables (page 200),
WHITMAN'S Candy Assortment, Mini Reubens (page 191), Mexi-Peanuts (page 191)

194

TACO CHICKEN WINGS

18 to 20 appetizers

**2 ¹/₂ pounds chicken wings
2 cups bread crumbs
1 package (1 ¹/₄ ounces)
OLD EL PASO Taco
Seasoning
1 jar (16 ounces) OLD EL
PASO Taco Sauce**

Cut chicken wings at joints, discarding tips. Combine bread crumbs and taco seasoning; mix well. Preheat oven to 375°F. Dip each chicken piece in taco sauce; roll in bread crumbs; coat thoroughly. Place on lightly greased baking sheet. Bake 30 to 35 minutes.

PARTY CHICKEN WINGS

48 appetizers

**24 chicken wings
1 cup soy sauce
²/₃ cup apricot preserves
¹/₂ cup finely chopped green
onions
2 tablespoons red wine
vinegar
1 tablespoon vegetable oil
¹/₂ teaspoon AC'CENT Flavor
Enhancer
1 garlic clove, minced**

Cut chicken wings at joints, discarding tips. In small mixing bowl, combine soy sauce, preserves, green onions, vinegar, oil, AC'CENT, and garlic; mix well. Place chicken wings in shallow baking dish and pour sauce mixture over wings. Cover and refrigerate 6 to 8 hours or overnight. Preheat oven to 400°F. Remove wings from marinade and place in single layer on jelly-roll pan. Bake 15 minutes. Turn and bake an additional 15 minutes.

CHICKEN CELERY SNACK

16 snacks

**1 package (3 ounces) cream
cheese, softened
1 can (4³/₄ ounces)
UNDERWOOD Chunky
Chicken Spread
¹/₄ teaspoon mild curry
powder
16 pieces celery (2-inch
pieces)
Paprika**

In small mixing bowl, mix cream cheese, chicken spread, and curry powder. Blend ingredients until smooth and creamy. Spread creamy chicken filling on celery pieces. Garnish stuffed celery with a sprinkle of paprika. Refrigerate until well chilled. Serve cold.

NOTE: *For ease in filling, pastry bag may be used.*

195

t's Have a Party! Let's Have a Party! Let's

PARTY CHICKEN PUFFS
Approximately 24 puffs

1 can (4³/₄ ounces)
  UNDERWOOD Chunky
  Chicken Spread
2 tablespoons shredded
  American cheese
1 tablespoon cream cheese,
  softened
2 teaspoons chopped green
  onion
¹/₂ teaspoon AC'CENT Flavor
  Enhancer
1 package (10 ounces) frozen
  pastry shells, thawed

Preheat oven to 400°F. In small bowl, mix all ingredients except pastry shells. On lightly floured board, line up pastry shells, overlapping edges slightly. With rolling pin, lightly roll over shells to form a single strip of pastry. Cut rounds of pastry with 3-inch round cutter. Place 1 scant teaspoon filling on each round; moisten edges of pastry with water, fold over filling and seal well. Place turnovers on ungreased cookie sheet and bake 15 to 20 minutes or until golden brown.

TANGY RIBLETS
30 appetizers

1¹/₂ to 2 pounds baby back
  pork ribs, cut length of
  slab by butcher
  Vegetable oil
1 garlic clove, minced
¹/₄ cup soy sauce
¹/₄ cup sherry
¹/₄ cup cider vinegar
¹/₂ cup firmly packed brown
  sugar
1 tablespoon cornstarch
³/₄ teaspoon AC'CENT Flavor
  Enhancer

Cut ribs into individual pieces. In wok or deep frying pan, heat oil to 360°F. Fry ribs 3 to 4 minutes or until meat is no longer pink. Drain on paper towels. In skillet, combine garlic, soy sauce, sherry, vinegar, brown sugar, cornstarch, and AC'CENT; bring to a boil. Add fried ribs and simmer 5 minutes, turning ribs to coat. Serve hot, with sauce if desired.

196

Let's Have a Party! Let's Have a Party! Let's Have a Party! Let's Have a Party! Let's Ha

BEEF AND BEAN EMPANADAS
50 empañadas

5 PET-RITZ Deep Dish
  Pie Crust Shells
¹/₂ pound lean ground beef
1 medium onion, chopped
¹/₂ cup OLD EL PASO Mild
      Taco Sauce or Tomatoes
      and Green Chilies
1 cup OLD EL PASO Refried
      Beans, any variety
¹/₂ teaspoon salt
¹/₄ teaspoon freshly ground
      black pepper
  PET Evaporated Milk
  OLD EL PASO Taco Sauce
      or OLD EL PASO Picante
      Salsa

Remove pie crust shells from freezer. Invert onto waxed paper. Let thaw until flat. Meanwhile, in large skillet, brown ground beef and onion. Drain fat. Add taco sauce or tomatoes and green chilies, refried beans, salt, and pepper. Heat; set aside and cool to room temperature. Roll each pie crust on lightly floured surface to 12-inch circle. With biscuit cutter, cut each crust into ten 2½-inch circles. Preheat oven to 400°F. Spoon 1 teaspoon cooled filling onto one side of each pastry circle. Fold pastry over filling. Seal edges with tines of fork. Place on well-greased cookie sheets. Brush with evaporated milk. Bake 15 to 20 minutes or until lightly browned. Serve with taco sauce or picante salsa.

NOTE: *Reroll scraps of pie crust dough to make additional empañadas. Empañadas can be made ahead and frozen. Reheat before serving.*

FRIED TOMATOES
Approximately 16 fried tomato slices

4 medium-size, firm
      (half-ripe) tomatoes
¹/₂ cup all-purpose flour
2 ¹/₂ teaspoons sugar
2 ¹/₂ teaspoons salt
¹/₄ teaspoon freshly ground
      black pepper
³/₄ cup PET Evaporated Milk
  Oil for frying

Wash tomatoes and cut into ½-inch slices. Drain tomato slices on paper towels. Combine flour, sugar, salt, and pepper. Dust tomato slices in flour mixture on both sides. Add evaporated milk to remaining flour mixture to form a thin batter. Dip floured tomato slices in batter. Fry in one inch hot oil until golden brown on both sides.

STUFFED JALAPENOS
20 to 22 appetizers

2 jars (10¼ ounces each) OLD EL PASO Whole Jalapeño Peppers
1 can (10½ ounces) OLD EL PASO Bean Dip
1 can (4¾ ounces) UNDERWOOD Chunky Chicken Spread
1 cup (4 ounces) shredded Cheddar cheese
½ cup PET Sour Cream

Preheat oven to 300°F. Drain, halve, seed, and rinse jalapeños. Drain again on paper towels. Mix bean dip and chicken spread. Stuff peppers with bean mixture. Sprinkle with cheese. Place on baking sheet. Bake 5 to 10 minutes or until cheese is bubbly. To serve, top with sour cream.

NACHOS
6 to 8 servings

1 box (7½ ounces) OLD EL PASO NACHIPS Tortilla Chips
1 can (16 ounces) OLD EL PASO Refried Beans, any variety
1 can (4 ounces) OLD EL PASO Chopped Green Chilies, or 1 jar (11¼ ounces) OLD EL PASO Jalapeño Slices
2½ cups (10 ounces) shredded Cheddar or Monterey Jack cheese

On a large baking sheet, spread tortilla chips. Top each with beans, and a few green chilies or 1 slice of jalapeño. Sprinkle each with 1 tablespoon cheese. Place under broiler 2 to 3 minutes or just until cheese melts. Serve immediately.

MICROWAVE DIRECTIONS: Microwave on HIGH 2 to 3 minutes or until cheese melts. Time will vary with the number of nachos prepared.

198

Let's Have a Party! Let's Have a Party! Let's Have a Party! Let's Have a Party! Let's Ha

Teen Party Menu:

Fresh Fruit Tray
Beef Tacos (page 126)
OLD EL PASO Frozen Chimichangas
topped with your choice of
Shredded Lettuce   Diced Tomatoes
Shredded Cheddar Cheese
PET Sour Cream   Guacamole (page 201)
OLD EL PASO Taco Sauce
OLD EL PASO Picante Salsa
OLD EL PASO Frozen Enchiladas
OLD EL PASO Spanish Rice
OLD EL PASO NACHIPS Tortilla Chips
Chilled Lemonade
Cinnamon Crisp (page 24)   PET Vanilla Ice Cream

TEEN PARTY

a) Dinner Plates b) OLD EL PASO Frozen Enchiladas
c) OLD EL PASO Frozen Chimichangas d) Beef Tacos
e) OLD EL PASO Spanish Rice
f) OLD EL PASO NACHIPS Tortilla Chips
g) Shredded Lettuce h) Shredded Cheddar Cheese
i) Diced Tomatoes j) PET Sour Cream k) Guacamole
l) OLD EL PASO Taco Sauce m) OLD EL PASO Picante Salsa
n) Fresh Fruit Tray o) Flatware and Napkins

OLD EL PASO Frozen Chimichangas, Beef Tacos (page 126)
OLD EL PASO Spanish Rice, OLD EL PASO NACHIPS Tortilla Chips

200

Let's Have a Party! Let's Have a Party! Let's Have a Party! Let's Have a Party! Let's Ha

CHEESY SHRIMP DIP

3¼ cups

1 can (4¼ ounces) ORLEANS
   Deveined Medium or
   Small Shrimp
½ cup chopped onions
2 tablespoons vegetable oil
1 can (10 ounces) OLD EL
   PASO Tomatoes and
   Green Chilies
4 cups (1 pound) cubed
   process American
   cheese
   Dash cayenne pepper
   OLD EL PASO NACHIPS
   Tortilla Chips

Rinse shrimp in cold running water. Drain. Sauté onions in hot oil until translucent. Stir in tomatoes and green chilies. Heat to steaming. Add cheese cubes, cook and stir over low heat until cheese is smooth and melted. Stir in shrimp and cayenne pepper. Serve warm with chips.

MICROWAVE DIRECTIONS: *Combine all ingredients except tortilla chips in microwave safe bowl. Microwave, uncovered, on 50% POWER 6 minutes or until heated through. Stir every 2 minutes.*

SPICY CHEESE DIP

2½ cups dip

(photograph on page 193)

2 cups PET Sour Cream
1 cup (4 ounces) shredded
   Cheddar cheese
¼ cup diced onion
¼ cup minced green pepper
¼ cup OLD EL PASO Taco
   Sauce or OLD EL PASO
   Picante Salsa
2 tablespoons OLD EL
   PASO Chopped Green
   Chilies
¼ teaspoon salt
   OLD EL PASO NACHIPS
   Tortilla Chips or
   assorted fresh
   vegetables

In medium bowl, mix all ingredients except NACHIPS Tortilla Chips or vegetables until well blended. Cover and refrigerate about 1 hour or until well chilled. Serve chilled dip with chips or fresh vegetables.

CHILI CON QUESO

2¼ cups dip

4 cups (1 pound) shredded process American cheese
1 can (10 ounces) OLD EL PASO Tomatoes and Green Chilies
1 box (7½ ounces) OLD EL PASO NACHIPS Tortilla Chips

In small saucepan, combine cheese and tomatoes and green chilies. Cook and stir over medium heat until cheese is smooth and melted. Serve warm with NACHIPS Tortilla Chips.

MICROWAVE DIRECTIONS: *Microwave, uncovered, on 50% POWER 8 to 10 minutes or until heated through. Stir every 2 minutes.*

GUACAMOLE

Approximately 2 cups guacamole   *(photograph on page 145)*

2 large ripe avocados, peeled, pitted, and sliced
1 jar (8 ounces) OLD EL PASO Taco Sauce or 1 cup OLD EL PASO Picante Salsa
½ cup chopped onions
2 tablespoons lemon or lime juice
1 teaspoon salt
½ teaspoon garlic powder
1 box (7½ ounces) OLD EL PASO NACHIPS Tortilla Chips

In blender or food processor, blend avocado slices, taco sauce or picante salsa, onions, juice, salt, and garlic powder until smooth. Chill. Serve with NACHIPS Tortilla Chips.

202

Let's Have a Party! Let's Have a Party! Let's Have a Party! Let's Have a Party! Let's Hav

HOLIDAY CHEESE BALL

One 3-inch cheese ball

2 cups (8 ounces) shredded Cheddar cheese
1 cup (4 ounces) grated Parmesan cheese
5 tablespoons crumbled Blue cheese
1 package (3 ounces) cream cheese, softened
1/2 teaspoon dry mustard
1 small can (5.33 fluid ounces) Pet Evaporated Milk
1 cup chopped pecans or walnuts

Beat together cheeses, dry mustard, and evaporated milk. Chill 1 hour or until firm. Shape into a ball. Roll in chopped nuts. Wrap in waxed paper. Chill until ready to serve. Serve with crackers.

DILLY SHRIMP CHEESE BALL

One 3-inch shrimp cheese ball

1 can (4 1/4 ounces) ORLEANS Deveined Broken Shrimp
1 package (8 ounces) cream cheese, softened
1 cup (4 ounces) shredded Cheddar cheese
2 tablespoons finely chopped onion
1 teaspoon AC'CENT Flavor Enhancer
1/4 teaspoon hot pepper sauce
1/4 teaspoon dillweed
1/8 teaspoon salt
1 cup chopped nuts

Rinse shrimp under cold running water. Drain. Combine remaining ingredients except nuts. Stir in shrimp. Chill. Shape into ball. Roll cheese ball in nuts, cover with waxed paper, and refrigerate until ready to serve.

NORWAY CHEESE BALLS

30 appetizers

2 cans (3¾ ounces each) UNDERWOOD Sardines, any variety
1 package (8 ounces) cream cheese, softened
2 teaspoons Worcestershire sauce
⅛ teaspoon freshly ground black pepper
1 cup finely chopped nuts

Drain sardines well and mash with fork. Add cream cheese, Worcestershire sauce, and pepper. Mix until smooth. Place in refrigerator. When mixture is well chilled, form into small balls about ¾ inch in diameter and roll in nuts. Cover. Chill and serve.

JALEPENO CHEESE BALL

One 3-inch cheese ball or
55 to 60 individual balls

(photograph on page 187)

3 OLD EL PASO Jalapeño Peppers
4 cups (1 pound) shredded sharp Cheddar cheese
1 large onion, quartered
3 garlic cloves, minced
½ cup mayonnaise
1 cup finely chopped pecans
OLD EL PASO NACHIPS Tortilla Chips

Remove tops and seeds from peppers. In food processor or grinder, grind together peppers, cheese, onion, and garlic. Mix in mayonnaise. Chill mixture until firm. Form chilled mixture into 1 large ball or many individual bite-size balls. Roll in pecans. Cover and refrigerate until ready to serve. Serve with NACHIPS Tortilla Chips.

The Cattle Paddle

One shipment of Holstein dairy cattle arriving in 1928 at a PET Milk condensary in Tennessee almost met a wet demise. Unloaded onto a green field beside the Nolichucky River, the weary herd plunged into the deep waters. The agent responsible for them left the scene in despair, convinced the floundering cows would drown. But cows are good swimmers. One found a footing on the steep mud banks, climbed up, and led the entire herd to safety.

FESTIVE CHEESE LOAF

24 servings

**2 packages (¹/₄ ounce each)
    active dry yeast**
2¹/₂ teaspoons sugar
**¹/₄ cup warm water
    (110°F to 115°F)**
**1 small can (5.33 fluid
    ounces) PET Evaporated
    Milk**
¹/₃ cup water
**3¹/₂ to 4 cups all-purpose
    flour**
**¹/₂ cup butter or margarine,
    softened**
2 teaspoons salt
**8 cups (2 pounds) shredded
    Muenster cheese**
**1 can (4 ounces) OLD EL
    PASO Chopped Green
    Chilies**
1 egg
**2 tablespoons ground
    coriander**

In large mixing bowl, dissolve yeast and sugar in ¼ cup warm water. In small saucepan, combine evaporated milk and ⅓ cup water. Heat to 110°F. Add to yeast mixture. Slowly beat in flour, butter, and salt. Cover and let rise in warm, draft-free place 1 hour or until doubled in bulk. Roll out on floured board to a circle about 18 inches in diameter. Preheat oven to 400°F. Combine cheese, green chilies, egg, and coriander. Place in center of dough. Fold in edge of dough, pleating edge over filling as you go, leaving a 2- to 3-inch center of cheese visible. Loaf should now be about 9-inches in diameter. Gently slide greased cookie sheet under filled loaf. Cover and let rise in warm, draft-free place 1 hour. Bake 30 to 35 minutes or until golden brown. Cool 15 minutes before serving. Slice in small wedges to serve.

This cheese-filled bread will bring ''ohs'' and ''ahs'' at a party.

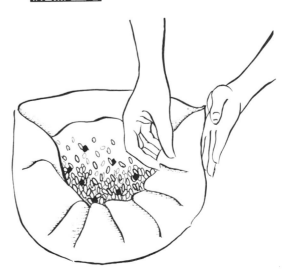

Festive Cheese Loaf

Breakfast Buffet Menu:
Chilled Orange Juice

Ham 'n' Swiss In A Shell (page 59)

Sausage

Fresh Fruit Compote   PET Sour Cream

DOWNYFLAKE Pancakes

Apple Nut Loaves (page 17)

AUNT FANNY'S Assorted Bakery Goods

Maple Syrup   Jam

Butter

Coffee

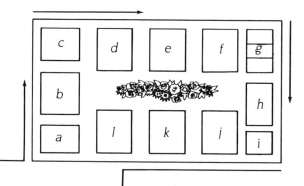

BREAKFAST BUFFET
a) Plates b) Ham 'n' Swiss In A Shell c) Sausage
d) DOWNYFLAKE Pancakes e) Apple Nut Loaves
f) Butter and Syrup g) Assorted Jam
h) Fresh Fruit Compote i) PET Sour Cream
j) AUNT FANNY'S Assorted Bakery Goods
k) Orange Juice and Coffee l) Flatware and Napkins

Ham 'n' Swiss in a Shell Company Style (page 59),
DOWNYFLAKE Pancakes, Miniature Apple Nut Loaf (page 17)

208

Let's Have a Party! Let's Have a Party! Let's Have a Party! Let's Have a Party! Let's Ha

BEEF CHILI CHEESE BRAID

1 loaf *(photograph on page 187)*

2³/₄ to 3 cups all-purpose flour, divided usage
1 package (¹/₄ ounce) active dry yeast
³/₄ cup water
2 tablespoons butter or margarine
1 tablespoon sugar
¹/₂ teaspoon salt
1 egg
2 tablespoons butter or margarine, melted
¹/₂ teaspoon crushed dried fine herbes
1 can (4 ounces) OLD EL PASO Chopped Green Chilies
¹/₂ cup (2 ounces) shredded Swiss cheese
¹/₂ cup (2 ounces) snipped thinly sliced smoked beef

In large mixing bowl, combine 1 cup flour and yeast. In saucepan, heat water, butter, sugar and salt just until warm (115°F to 120°F), stirring constantly until butter almost melts. Add water mixture, along with egg, to flour mixture. Beat with electric mixer on LOW for 30 seconds. Beat on HIGH for 3 minutes. Stir in as much of the remaining flour as needed to form stiff dough. On floured board, knead about 5 minutes until smooth and elastic. Cover. Let rest 10 minutes. On lightly floured surface, roll dough out to 12 × 9-inch rectangle. Cut dough lengthwise into three 12 × 3-inch strips. Brush strips with some of the melted butter; sprinkle with fine herbes. Sprinkle a third of green chilies, cheese and beef lengthwise down center of each strip. To form long ropes, pinch together edges. Place ropes side-by-side on large greased cookie sheet, seam-side down. Braid ropes together and pinch ends. Cover. Let dough rise about 30 minutes or until nearly doubled in bulk. Preheat oven to 375°F. Bake 25 to 30 minutes or until loaf is golden brown and sounds hollow when lightly tapped. Brush loaf with remaining melted butter and sprinkle with additional crushed fine herbes. Serve warm.

MUSHROOM QUICHE

6 to 8 servings as main dish
12 servings as appetizers

(photograph on page 187)

4 eggs
1 1/2 cups PET Whipping Cream
1 teaspoon salt, divided
   usage
1/8 teaspoon ground nutmeg
1 cup (4 ounces) shredded
   Swiss cheese
1/4 cup butter or margarine
1/2 pound mushrooms, thinly
   sliced
2 tablespoons chopped green
   onion
1/8 teaspoon freshly ground
   black pepper
1 PET-RITZ Deep Dish
   Pie Crust Shell

Preheat oven and cookie sheet to 375°F. In medium bowl, mix eggs, cream, ¾ teaspoon salt, and nutmeg with wire whisk. Stir in cheese. In medium skillet, melt butter. Add mushrooms, green onion, remaining ¼ teaspoon salt, and pepper. Cook about 5 minutes or until vegetables are tender, stirring often. Stir mushroom mixture into cream mixture. Pour into pie crust. Bake on preheated cookie sheet 35 to 40 minutes or until knife inserted in center comes out clean. Cool 10 minutes before serving.

SHRIMP COCKTAIL

6 servings

3 cans (4 1/4 ounces each)
   ORLEANS Deveined
   Medium or Large Shrimp
Chopped ice

Rinse shrimp under cold running water. Drain. Fill bowl with chopped ice and arrange shrimp over ice. Place small dish in center of shrimp bowl and fill with Cocktail Sauce. Provide toothpicks for handy dipping.

COCKTAIL SAUCE

6 servings

1 cup chili sauce
1/2 cup finely chopped celery
1 1/2 tablespoons lemon juice
1 1/2 tablespoons horseradish
1/2 teaspoon salt

Combine all ingredients and chill.

210

Let's Have a Party! Let's Have a Party! Let's Have a Party! Let's Have a Party! Let's Ha

Dinner Menu:

Shrimp Cocktail with Cocktail Sauce (page 209)

Beef Birds (page 42)

Fluffy Mashed Potatoes (page 44)

Glazed Carrots (page 54)

Creamy Cucumber Salad (page 97)

HEARTLAND Rolls (page 25)   Whipped Butter

Burgundy or Bordeaux Wine

Coffee Liqueur Pie (page 214)

Café Au Lait (page 92)

FORMAL DINNER

a) Napkin b) Dinner Plate c) Cocktail Glass and Liner Plate
d) Salad Plate e) Water Goblet f) Wine Goblet
g) Dinner Fork h) Salad Fork i) Dessert Fork* j) Knife
k) Teaspoon l) Seafood Fork

*The dessert fork may be placed at the setting, or
 brought with dessert.

It took a little girl and a family heirloom to inspire the creation of an American marketing classic. Walter Sharp, the third president of Stephen F. Whitman and Son, had often admired the beautiful and intricate stitched sampler that hung in his home. The little girl whose months of slow, precise, painstaking effort produced the heirloom had been Sharp's own grandmother. One day Sharp was struck with a brilliant idea: what could be more elegant than a candy box bearing that same charming sampler design? The cross-stitch pattern was lovingly duplicated, right down to the Belgian linen texture, and the WHITMAN'S SAMPLER was born.

Its name bore a dual meaning, thanks to another touch of marketing genius. The WHITMAN'S SAMPLER was the first box of candy to come with its own index — a much-appreciated diagram in the box lid. "Now," gloated company salesmen, "people won't have to poke their fingers into a chocolate to see what's inside."

Sharp's creative touch would have pleased his company's innovative founder. Sixty years earlier, Stephen Whitman had opened a small "confectioner and fruiterer" shop near Philadelphia's bustling waterfront. It was a happy choice of location — sailors and ship captains were willing

couriers of the hard-to-find imported fruits, nuts, cocoa, and flavoring oils Whitman needed for his little shop to compete with the famous French candymakers. Soon Whitman's candies were the darling of Philadelphia's carriage trade.

The growing company's reputation was spread by pleased customers who dropped in to browse among their favorite confections or to order their own special assortments. The only packaged candy ever produced by Stephen Whitman, a pink-and-gilt affair called "Choice Mixed Sugarplums from Stephen F. Whitman," was among the first packaged confections in printed boxes, and was at the forefront of today's trademarked packaging.

Stephen Whitman had a marketing instinct unusual in his day. He placed his first newspaper ad before the Civil War, and the company was advertising regularly in magazines before the turn of the century.

But it was Walter Sharp who took the firm from regional business to national enterprise. His WHITMAN'S SAMPLER quickly became the best-known and best-selling box of prestige candy in America. Sharp also brought us

the famous Whitman's "art" tins — "Salmagundi," "Pleasure Island," the "Prestige" — that have become prized collector's items.

The all-American soda fountain was in its heyday in the 1920s and '30s, and Whitman's produced syrups, sauces, and icings to enhance the sodas and sundaes. The famous Whitman's MESSENGER BOY made his appearance in that era, to become a well-known symbol for Whitman's candies. And almost every major movie star of the 1930s was featured in Whitman's ads in the *Saturday Evening Post* — endorsements that would be worth thousands today. Compensation in those days: several boxes of Whitman's Chocolates!

A popular Whitman's slogan penned in that era acknowledged the role of the candy box in romance — "A woman never forgets the man who remembers." Whitman's continued its matchmaking role in World War II, when more than six million pounds of its candy were sent to soldiers overseas. The young women on the packing lines sometimes slipped their names and addresses into the candy tins, resulting in correspondences that, for some, led to marriage.

A large, modern plant on the fringes of Greater Philadelphia is the site of candy production today. Shortly after that new plant opened in 1961, Whitman's wonderful products came to Pet. The charming sense of Americana brought by the WHITMAN'S SAMPLER and the company's other beloved confections has enriched us all, and that product line has continued to grow. The Whitman's Division of Pet Incorporated now markets a broad line of confectionery products, including chocolates for home enjoyment or gift-giving, chocolate chips, baking chocolate, hard candy sticks, Danish butter cookies, special items for Easter and Christmas, and, of course, Valentine hearts.

Many years have passed since a gentleman caller to Stephen Whitman's little candy shop could ponder over the perfect selection to win his ladylove, but it's just as true today as it was then — the quickest way to a chocolate lover's heart is a romantic Whitman's Valentine.

214

Let's Have a Party! Let's Have a Party! Let's Have a Party! Let's Have a Party! Let's Ha

CHOCOLATE FONDUE

6 to 8 servings   *(photograph on page 187)*

**2 bars (8 ounces each) milk
    chocolate**
**1 small can (5.33 fluid
    ounces) PET Evaporated
    Milk**
¹/₈ teaspoon salt
**3 tablespoons creme de
    cacao or orange-flavored
    liqueur**

In medium saucepan over low heat, combine chocolate, evaporated milk, and salt. Cook about 5 minutes or until thickened, stirring constantly. Stir in liqueur. Pour into fondue pot, and keep warm.

Dippers: *angel cake, pound cake, maraschino cherries, apples, pears, marshmallows, bananas, or strawberries.*

COFFEE LIQUEUR PIE

8 servings

**1 small can (5.33 fluid
    ounces) PET Evaporated
    Milk**
**¹/₂ cup (3 ounces) WHITMAN'S
    Semi-Sweet Chocolate
    Chips**
**2 cups miniature
    marshmallows**
**¹/₃ cup chopped toasted
    almonds**
¹/₃ cup coffee liqueur
**1 container (12 ounces)
    PET WHIP Non-Dairy
    Whipped Topping,
    thawed**
**1 PET-RITZ Regular Pie Crust
    Shell, baked**
  **Pet Whip Non-Dairy
    Whipped Topping,
    thawed**
  Chopped almonds
  Maraschino cherries

In heavy 1-quart saucepan, combine evaporated milk and chocolate chips. Cook over low heat, stirring occasionally, until chocolate melts completely and mixture thickens. Stir in marshmallows until melted. Remove from heat. Add almonds. Pour into 2-quart bowl and refrigerate 20 to 30 minutes or until cool, stirring twice. Add coffee liqueur. Fold in one container PET WHIP. Spoon into baked pie crust. Freeze several hours or until firm. Remove from freezer 10 minutes before serving for ease in cutting. Garnish with additional PET WHIP, chopped almonds, and maraschino cherries.

To toast almonds: *Place almonds on baking sheet in preheated 350°F oven and bake about 10 minutes or until almonds are lightly toasted, stirring frequently.*

FUDGE NUT LOG

Approximately 3 dozen slices

1 cup firmly packed brown sugar
1/4 cup light corn syrup
1/4 cup PET Evaporated Milk
1 1/2 teaspoons vanilla
1 cup (6 ounces) WHITMAN'S Semi-Sweet Chocolate Chips
3 cups chopped pecans, divided usage

In 1½-quart saucepan, combine brown sugar, syrup, and evaporated milk. Bring to a full boil, stirring constantly, and boil 2 to 3 minutes. Remove from heat. Beat in vanilla. Add chocolate chips and 1½ cups pecans. Stir until chocolate melts. Beat with wire whisk until smooth. Divide chocolate mixture in half and form 2 logs. Roll each log separately in remaining 1½ cups pecans. Wrap logs in waxed paper. Refrigerate 2½ to 3 hours or until firm. To serve, cut logs into ½-inch slices.

ICE CREAM CRUNCH BALLS

8 ice cream balls

2 cups crushed chocolate sandwich cookies (about 24 cookies)
1 cup finely chopped pecans
1 cup slivered almonds
1 teaspoon peppermint extract
1 container (1/2 gallon) PET Vanilla Ice Cream, firm

Combine cookie crumbs and nuts. Add peppermint extract and mix well. Pour generous amount of mixture onto waxed paper. Scoop ½ cup vanilla ice cream onto crumb mixture. Roll quickly and firmly into a ball, covering ice cream completely with crumbs. Place ice cream ball in foil cupcake liner. Repeat procedure until 8 ice cream balls have been formed. Freeze about 1 hour or until firm.

NOTE: *If ice cream becomes soft, return to freezer 30 minutes before reshaping.*

What's in a Name?

"A Woman Never Forgets the Man Who Remembers" was one of the famous advertising slogans created for the WHITMAN'S SAMPLER in the 1930s. It was a distinct improvement over an earlier slogan, "The Fussy Package for Fastidious Folks."

216

Let's Have a Party! Let's Have a Party! Let's Have a Party! Let's Have a Party! Let's Ha

CREAMY EGGNOG
2 quarts

6 eggs
²/₃ cup sugar
¹/₄ teaspoon salt
2 tall cans (12 ounces each)
     PET Evaporated Milk
2 cups PET Whipping Cream
¹/₄ cup vanilla
2 to 3 tablespoons rum
     flavoring, or ¹/₂ cup rum
   Ground nutmeg or
     cinnamon

In 3-quart mixing bowl, beat together eggs, sugar, and salt. Add evaporated milk, cream, vanilla, and rum; mix until well blended. Chill. Pour into punch bowl. Sprinkle with nutmeg or cinnamon.

VARIATION: *For a lighter eggnog, use* PET *Light Cream in place of whipping cream.*

HOLIDAY CLUSTERS
30 clusters

1 cup sugar
1 small can (5.33 fluid
     ounces) PET Evaporated
     Milk
1 cup (6 ounces) WHITMAN'S
     Semi-Sweet Chocolate
     Chips
1 tablespoon butter or
     margarine
1 cup HEARTLAND Natural
     Cereal, Plain, Raisin, or
     Coconut

In saucepan, combine sugar and evaporated milk. Bring to a full boil. Heat and stir 2 additional minutes. Remove from heat. Stir in chocolate chips and butter until chocolate is completely melted. Stir in HEARTLAND cereal. Drop by teaspoonfuls onto waxed paper. Chill until firm.

MICROWAVE COOKING CHART
Remove all canned products from can to microwave safe dish

PRODUCT	AMOUNT	POWER	TIME	SPECIAL INSTRUCTIONS
OLD EL PASO Refried Beans	8¼ oz. 15-16 oz.	FULL POWER FULL POWER	40-80 SECONDS 2-3 MINUTES	Cover. Turn 1 or 2 times during cooking period.
OLD EL PASO Chili Con Carne	15 oz.	FULL POWER	1½-2½ MINUTES	Cover. Turn 1 or 2 times during cooking period.
OLD EL PASO Chili with Beans	15 oz.	FULL POWER	1½-2½ MINUTES	Cover. Turn 1 or 2 times during cooking period.
OLD EL PASO Spanish Rice	15 oz.	FULL POWER	2-3 MINUTES	Cover. Turn 1 or 2 times during cooking period.
OLD EL PASO Beef Taco Filling	8¼ oz.	FULL POWER	50-90 SECONDS	Cover. Turn 1 or 2 times during cooking period.
OLD EL PASO Beef Enchiladas	6 enchiladas	FULL POWER	2½-3½ MINUTES	Cover. Turn 1 or 2 times during cooking period.
OLD EL PASO Tamales	6 tamales	FULL POWER	1½-2½ MINUTES	Cover. Turn 1 or 2 times during cooking period.
OLD EL PASO Frozen Enchiladas				Follow package directions.
OLD EL PASO Frozen Burrito	1 burrito	FULL POWER	1½-2½ MINUTES	Remove from package. Turn 1 or 2 times during cooking period.
DOWNYFLAKE Pancakes	2 pancakes 4 pancakes 8 pancakes	FULL POWER FULL POWER FULL POWER	1-1½ MINUTES 2½-3 MINUTES 3½-4 MINUTES	Remove pancakes from package and place on microwave safe plate.
DOWNYFLAKE French Toast	1 slice 3 slices 6 slices	FULL POWER FULL POWER FULL POWER	1-1¼ MINUTES 2-2¼ MINUTES 3½-4 MINUTES	Remove French toast from package and place on microwave safe plate.
COMPLIMENT White Sauce	13.3 oz.	FULL POWER	2½-3½ MINUTES	Serve heated sauce over meat, noodles, or vegetables.
HEARTLAND Natural Cereal	½ cup	FULL POWER	2 MINUTES	Add ½ cup water. Microwave. Cover and let stand 1 to 2 minutes. Serve with brown sugar and cinnamon.
PET-RITZ Pie Crust Shell*	1 shell	FULL POWER	4-6 MINUTES	Transfer to microwave safe pie plate; let stand until thawed. Mold to plate; prick with fork. Microwave until crust no longer looks doughy.

*Pie shells must always be precooked for pies cooked in the microwave.

INDEX FOR MICROWAVE RECIPES

NOTE: *A few products included in this book are distributed regionally and may not be available in your area.*

INDEX